Julie
Rayburn

Peace
in the
Storms
of Life

*Devotional Encouragement
for Women*

BARBOUR BOOKS
An Imprint of Barbour Publishing, Inc.

Published by Barbour Books, an imprint of Barbour Publishing, Inc., 1810 Barbour Drive, Uhrichsville, Ohio 44683, www.barbourbooks.com

Our mission is to inspire the world with the life-changing message of the Bible.

Member of the
Evangelical Christian
Publishers Association

Printed in China.

God is our refuge and strength,
a very present help in trouble.
Therefore we will not fear
though the earth gives way,
though the mountains be moved
into the heart of the sea.

PSALM 46:1–2

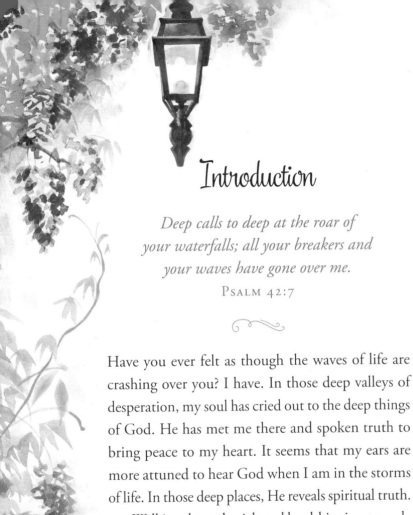

Introduction

*Deep calls to deep at the roar of
your waterfalls; all your breakers and
your waves have gone over me.*

PSALM 42:7

Have you ever felt as though the waves of life are
crashing over you? I have. In those deep valleys of
desperation, my soul has cried out to the deep things
of God. He has met me there and spoken truth to
bring peace to my heart. It seems that my ears are
more attuned to hear God when I am in the storms
of life. In those deep places, He reveals spiritual truth.

Walking through trials and hardships is extremely
difficult. Yet the storms in my life have proven to be
pivotal times of spiritual growth as I have clung to the
Lord for peace and strength. My desire is to pass on
what the Lord has taught me in hopes that you also

4

might be encouraged by God's Word. These devotionals and questions reflect God's challenges to my own heart. Unfortunately, some of my storms have been of my own making. As you meditate on scripture and reflect upon the questions after each devotional, I hope you will journal your thoughts and personal reflections. Go through this book alone or with a group. Take your time as you cry out to Him from the depths of your soul. God will be faithful to meet you in those deep waters.

My eternal gratitude to my Good Shepherd, who has been with me through every storm and carried me to the other side; to Community Bible Study, for imparting a passion for God's Word; to Scott, my husband and best friend, for your constant love and support; to my children Jenn and Thomas, daughter-in-law Kelley, and grandchildren Karyssa, Alex, Samantha, and Jackson, I am so blessed to have each one of you in my life; to Sue Westrum's inspiring legacy as a Wycliffe missionary; to Ann, a reader who encouraged me to write again after sharing how God used *Be Still and Know* to minister to her; to the Barbour Publishing family, for your support over the years; to all my readers, family, and friends who have been with me on this journey and helped me persevere—you know who you are!

The Unexpected

"Fear not, for I have redeemed you; I have called you by name, you are mine. When you pass through the waters, I will be with you; and through the rivers, they shall not overwhelm you; when you walk through fire you shall not be burned, and the flame shall not consume you. For I am the LORD your God, the Holy One of Israel, your Savior."

ISAIAH 43:1–3

Unfortunately, life is full of the unexpected. Sudden heart palpitations result in an emergency room visit in the middle of the night. An engagement means a cross-country move. A hurricane wreaks havoc as it barrels onshore. Out of the blue we can find ourselves overwhelmed and anxious. Stress causes our pulse to increase and blood pressure to rise. Fear takes over. Our sympathetic nervous system kicks in for a fight or flight response!

Even in the unexpected events of life, God tells us to "fear not." Why? Although we may not know where life's journey will take us, we can be assured that He walks beside us every step of the way. Peace and strength are available to us through the indwelling Holy Spirit, God's presence. Philippians 4:6–7 assures us that when we bring our anxiety to the Lord through prayer with thanksgiving, His peace will guard our hearts (emotions) and minds (thoughts). What a promise!

When the road ahead looks ominous, focus on God walking beside you, not on the unknown future. "The joy of the LORD is your strength" (Nehemiah 8:10). "For he himself is our peace" (Ephesians 2:14). What great promises to cling to when the road gets rough. You have assurance that it will be all right, not because your life will work out according to your plan, but because your life is in His hands. Even on the difficult roads of life, God will carry you to the other side. Trust Him when the unexpected comes your way.

What unexpected life events have you experienced? What is your typical response, fight or flight? Read Philippians 4:6–7 if you are going through a difficult time right now.

Fix Your Eyes

*Looking to Jesus, the founder and perfecter of
our faith, who for the joy that was set before him
endured the cross, despising the shame, and is seated
at the right hand of the throne of God.*

HEBREWS 12:2

Maggie received her driver's permit and couldn't wait to get behind the wheel! One evening as she drove with her dad on a narrow two-lane, winding road, she was blinded by oncoming headlights. Her dad advised, "When the headlights are blinding you, fix your eyes on the white line on the right edge of the road. That's your guide. Keep the car to the left of that white line."

On the road of life, there are many lights and distractions that blind us and prevent us from staying in God's lane. The quest for material possessions can lead to greed. Eventually money can usurp the Lord's rightful place in our lives. So much time can be spent at jobs, pursuing hobbies, or with family and friends, that we have little time to read the Bible or pray. How do we stay on God's path? How do we stay in the center of His will for our lives?

Just as Maggie kept her eyes fixed on the white line, you need to fix your eyes on Jesus to prevent being sidetracked or running off the road. What does "fixing your eyes on Jesus" entail? Jesus is your focus, your first priority—not money, your job, your children, your family, or your hobbies. The truth found in His Word is the plumb line to live by. Read the Bible and apply what you learn. Set aside time to pray and ask for His wisdom, direction, and help. He is your focus. He is your white line. He will keep you from being spiritually blinded. Fix your eyes on Jesus and stay the course!

What are your eyes fixed on? Have you been able to stay the course? When you think about fixing your eyes on Jesus, what practical applications come to mind?

Name-Calling

"A new commandment I give to you, that you love one another: just as I have loved you, you also are to love one another. By this all people will know that you are my disciples, if you have love for one another."

JOHN 13:34–35

Children are notorious for calling each other names. They are quick to point out flaws and differences. They capitalize on one another's weaknesses. Adults should have left these childish antics behind, but perhaps they have just learned how to disguise their hate. Today, words such as "religious fanatic," "liberal elite," and "right-wing extremist" are tossed about routinely. People are labeled "stupid," "fat," and "gay." Name-calling only serves to hurt individuals and divide us all.

As Christians, we have our convictions. We believe the Bible is the Word of God—God's truth. We believe that since we are created by God, life is best lived according to His design. The owner's manual is the Bible. Nonbelievers may label Christians negatively and even persecute them. What is our response? Do we become angry and resort to calling them names in retaliation?

You alone are responsible for how you live. We are all accountable to God. You are not the judge of those around you, especially nonbelievers. Instead you are to be salt and light in their midst, pointing them to Jesus. They should see something compellingly different in you—and that "something different" is Jesus. Name-calling serves only to repel, not attract. Jesus said we would know His disciples by their love for one another. Name-calling is not an expression of love. The next time someone pins an unattractive name on you, turn the other cheek. Refrain from doing the same. When you set childish ways aside, they will be able to see the love of Jesus in your response and be drawn to Him.

Do you think Christians are just as guilty as nonbelievers in leveling attacks against one another? Explain. What are some practical ways to live out John 13:34–35? Now act on them.

Building Your House

"Everyone then who hears these words of mine and does them will be like a wise man who built his house on the rock."

MATTHEW 7:24

In Matthew 7:24–27, Jesus describes two houses representing our lives. One house is built on a rock foundation and the other on sand. Only the one built on rock withstood the rain, wind, and floods. The house built on sand suffered a mighty fall. Storms of life will come. The foundation we build our lives on determines whether we will stand victorious or fall in ruins. Victory is obtained through obedience to God's Word.

Marriages built around children will struggle. The Bible is clear that the marital relationship must come first. Chasing after material gain will leave us empty. The Bible exhorts us to store up treasures in heaven instead—to focus on eternal, not temporary things. Christians may know that the Bible is God's Word, but obeying truth is difficult to live out consistently.

How can you be wise and build your life so that it can

weather any adversity? Read the Bible on a daily basis and allow truth to penetrate your heart. Apply what you read. Profoundly simple, yet extremely difficult. Join a Bible study or small group to encourage you. Repent when you sin, and ask for the Lord's help. Realign your priorities. Seek His heart. Yield to the Holy Spirit's control on a moment-by-moment basis. When you start to get off course, listen to that still, small voice of God's warning. Submit to God's ways and not your own. "But seek first the kingdom of God and his righteousness, and all these things will be added to you" (Matthew 6:33). Build your life upon the Rock of Jesus Christ and you will stand!

As you look at the foundation of your life, what have you built your life on? How have you fared in the storms of life? It's difficult to read God's Word consistently. Joining an in-depth Bible study will help. Check out www.communitybiblestudy.org for a class near you.

Relationships

"I have loved you with an everlasting love; therefore I have continued my faithfulness to you."

JEREMIAH 31:3

Even though Israel had forsaken the Lord and worshipped other idols in rebellion, God declared His everlasting love toward them. They had been unfaithful, yet He remained faithful. Israel had sinned, yet God remained holy. God desired a close relationship with His chosen people, yet they turned away. God's love pursued and disciplined them for their own good in hopes that they would repent and turn back to Him.

Broken. Estranged. Toxic. These words can be used to describe relationships. Friends fall away. Couples get divorced. Children become estranged. Maintaining strong and therapeutic relationships requires the work of two imperfect people. But what if it were possible to have a relationship with someone who *is* perfect? What if they loved us unconditionally, even when we messed up? What if they always kept their end of the bargain even though we faltered? Would we want to be in that kind of relationship?

"Jesus Christ is the same yesterday and today and forever" (Hebrews 13:8). God loved Israel with an everlasting love, and He loves you with an everlasting love! He desires a personal relationship with you. You will never have to worry about God walking out or getting mad and not talking to you. He will never want out of the relationship. You will never be "unfriended" by God. Once we accept Jesus as our personal Lord and Savior, He is with us to stay! Wow! There is a saying, "If you don't feel close to God, guess who moved?" It's true. We can move away from God and turn our backs on Him, but He will never do that to us. Will you embrace the everlasting love of God? You can always feel secure in His love and faithfulness toward you.

Is your relationship with God close or distant? Why do you think so? Have you embraced God's unconditional love for you? Trust Him and receive His eternal love. If you have an intimate relationship with Jesus, how could you grow even closer?

Love Letters

For I am sure that neither death nor life,
nor angels nor rulers, nor things present nor things
to come, nor powers, nor height nor depth,
nor anything else in all creation, will be
able to separate us from the love of
God in Christ Jesus our Lord.

ROMANS 8:38–39

Since becoming empty nesters, Sue and Jim's lives had become very routine—work, eat dinner, watch TV, go to bed—repeat. Over time they began drifting apart. One day Sue came across a love letter that Jim had written to her on their twenty-fifth wedding anniversary. Jim recounted all of Sue's admirable qualities and described how rich his life had been because of her. Sue's love toward Jim was instantly rekindled, and she desired to cultivate their love by moving past the mundane.

We all enjoy receiving love letters. The Bible is God's love letter to us. He affirms that He loved us first (1 John 4:19). After Adam's fall in the Garden of Eden, God put a plan in motion to redeem us (Genesis 3:15). God would send Jesus to earth to be born, live, and then give up His life so that we could have eternal life. That's how much He loves us!

Emotions can be unreliable. You may feel down and conclude that God doesn't love you. That is never true! He always loves you. God never withdraws His love. It is unconditional, everlasting, and perfect. God will never leave or forsake you, and no one can ever snatch you out of His hand. He fights for you and protects you. God sets you free and gives you peace. His love is never selfish—He always wants the best for you. Don't let His love letter to you go unopened. Read about His great love for you in the Bible, and you will be encouraged and inspired to cultivate that love relationship.

Have you ever thought of the Bible as God's love letter to you? What verses are your favorites? Read the following verses and jot down what you glean: Psalm 86:15; John 3:16; Romans 5:8; Ephesians 2:4–5.

Little Judges

Therefore you have no excuse, O man, every one of you who judges. For in passing judgment on another you condemn yourself, because you, the judge, practice the very same things.

ROMANS 2:1

Little judges are everywhere. They evaluate drivers on the road, the parenting skills of others, and the boss's decisions. They judge people's motives and attitudes without knowing the facts. Even though they assess and critique others, they remain unaware of their own shortcomings. Who gave them the right to sit in judgment? What standards are they using? Although we loathe being judged, if we look in the mirror, we just may be face-to-face with a little judge ourselves.

Judging can become insidious and habitual. We may not realize that we've adopted a judgmental attitude because we disguise our comments. Even prayer requests are breeding grounds for passing judgment when we add our two cents. We measure people who are different from us according to our standards, and when they fall short, we judge. Beware! "There is only one lawgiver and judge, he who is able to save and to destroy. But who are you to judge your neighbor?" (James 4:12).

God is the only wise judge. Because He is holy and omniscient, His judgments are true and righteous. Remember the adulterous woman whom Jesus defended? (See John 8:1–11.) Those in the crowd were also guilty of sin. You are too. That's why you need to remove the log in your own eye first (see Matthew 7:1–5). Instead of being overly concerned with others, concentrate on your own walk with God. What things are not pleasing? What sins are you attempting to cover up? We are all accountable to God alone. Get your life in order before Him. Quit worrying about others, and allow Him to change your heart, attitude, and actions. Leave the judging to God.

Examine your attitude. Do you think that you are superior or inferior to others? There are many reasons why we sit in judgment. Ask God to expose your true motives. Then ask Him to help you overcome the temptation to judge.

Stand in the Storm

"Everyone then who hears these words of mine
and does them will be like a wise man who built
his house on the rock. And the rain fell, and
the floods came, and the winds blew and
beat on that house, but it did not fall,
because it had been founded on the rock."

MATTHEW 7:24–25

What are you building your life on? There are many choices at our disposal. We can build our lives around our families, jobs, homes, and hobbies. We can pursue pleasure, money, education, beauty, power, and prestige. It's inevitable: storms of life come to everyone. How we weather those storms will depend on our foundation. Unfortunately, the world's choice of building material is like shifting sand—unstable, uncertain, and collapsible. God has a better foundation in mind.

There's a children's song that contrasts the wise and foolish builder. The wise man built his house upon the rock, whereas the foolish man built his house upon the sand. When the rains descended on the house on sand, it went *smash!* Although children love to loudly clap their hands together, there is nothing funny about a shattered life.

Jesus states that a wise man (or woman) builds his house upon the rock. That Rock is Jesus Christ, the Chief Cornerstone. Jesus explains plainly that He becomes the foundation of your life when you hear His words and do them. You have a choice. You are foolish if you choose to build your life upon the sands of today's culture. When hardships and trials come, you will be destroyed. However, if you choose to pursue Jesus by reading His Word and living in obedience to it, you will stand firm when the unexpected storms of life attempt to knock you down. Build your life upon the firm and eternal Rock of Jesus Christ so that you will be able to stand in the storm!

What foundation are you building your life on? Would you say that you are using temporary or eternal building materials?

Love Compels

But God shows his love for us in that
while we were still sinners, Christ died for us.

ROMANS 5:8

In the beginning, God created a perfect world. He made lush, beautiful vegetation and picturesque scenery. God placed the moon and sun in their precise locations in the universe to sustain life. Animals, birds, and reptiles roamed together. Man was created to enjoy a love relationship with God. They freely walked and talked together in the garden. That was God's perfect design. Doesn't it sound wonderful?

We all know the "rest of the story." Sin entered the world and destroyed utopia. Adam and Eve chose to disobey God and hid when the guilt of their sin overwhelmed them. Relationships were marred as pain was ushered in. God's heart was broken. Yet love compelled Him to act. God Himself covered their naked bodies with animal skins. He then foretold of a Savior who would crush Satan forever. (See Genesis 1–3.)

Sin continues to wreak havoc in today's world. Sinful

choices not only affect you adversely, but their ripple effects can damage those in following generations. Divorce and child abuse can destroy lives. Even anger and pride bring people to ruin. God's heart is broken as He witnesses the pain that sin continues to cause. Like Adam and Eve, sometimes you may attempt to hide from God. To numb your guilt, you could turn to drugs, alcohol, sex, or other addictions. Or staying busy may prevent you from being alone with your thoughts. A downward spiral ensues as you are sucked further into despair. Who will intervene and save you from yourself? The same God who sought out Adam and Eve seeks you. Love still compels God to act. Christ died so that you could live. Repent. Turn around. Embrace the love of your heavenly Father today. There is no need to run and hide any longer. God loves you!

Ask God to expose any sin that may be present in your life, and then confess it. Receive His forgiveness. There is no sin that trumps His love! Love wins!

The Soldier's Sacrifice

Share in suffering as a good soldier of Christ Jesus.
2 TIMOTHY 2:3

Soldiers willingly sacrifice their lives to serve their country. The liberties we enjoy were bought at a high price by those who have gone before us. The cost was great—physically, mentally, and emotionally—yet they were willing. The debt can never be repaid. As we enjoy our freedom, let us remember with gratitude those who sacrificed on our behalf.

There is another battle that rages—a spiritual one. The apostles were on the front lines after Jesus' death and resurrection. They were arrested, beaten, and imprisoned. What if they had given up? What if they had caved? Would we know the freedom that we experience in Christ today? The apostles and Christians after them continued to "fight the good fight" so that Christ would be known throughout future generations (see 2 Timothy 4:7). All the disciples, with the exception of John, died a martyr's death. We know Jesus today because thousands of years ago they were willing to suffer for truth!

What about future generations? Will they come to know Jesus, the Prince of Peace? Will they be set free from the bondage of sin? You may not go to war or be imprisoned, yet you are called to suffer as a soldier of Christ so that the truth of the Gospel will live on. Whenever you choose to go God's way rather than the world's way, you will encounter opposition. However, truth must be lived out in your life so that others will see and come to believe. Read God's Word daily and apply what you learn. Persevere in your marriage. Love the prodigal. Speak the truth. Consider future generations. Are you willing to make the sacrifice for their spiritual freedom? Let's be inspired by the sacrifice of others so that we are willing to lay down our lives for the sake of Christ.

Have you or someone you know suffered for Christ? How might you "fight the good fight" for future generations? What steps might you take today?

Entering His Presence

Let us then with confidence draw near to the
throne of grace, that we may receive mercy
and find grace to help in time of need.

HEBREWS 4:16

When hard times come upon us, where do we flee? We may call a good friend who serves as a sounding board. Perhaps we try to drown the pain with alcohol. Or we may plunge into the pit of despair where depression overtakes our emotions. The Lord wants us to have victory. . .even in the midst of the most difficult situations. It is possible because of Jesus.

Jesus is our High Priest. Through faith in Him, we have been given access to our heavenly Father. What a rich promise! "For we do not have a high priest who is unable to sympathize with our weaknesses, but one who in every respect has been tempted as we are, yet without sin" (Hebrews 4:15). As a man, Jesus walked on earth and endured trials, temptations, and hardships. He experienced rejection, hatred, betrayal, insults, and pain. Yet because He was fully man and fully God, He never succumbed to sin. That is good news for us! His sinless life was sacrificed on our behalf, giving us eternal life. But that's not all. Since Jesus encountered human temptations and hardships yet emerged victorious, we too can experience victory through Him when hard times come upon us!

So instead of calling a friend or reaching for a glass of wine, enter His presence through prayer. Lay all your burdens, cares, and worries at His feet. Jesus understands. Confess your weakness to handle the situation. Jesus understands. Prayer is entering the very presence of God. When you spend time with Him, you will be changed. You will receive grace and mercy. You will experience peace that passes all understanding. Flee to Jesus, and enter His presence today!

Where do you turn for help when you feel overwhelmed with life? When you are going through difficult times, does God feel near or far away? Draw near to Him and He will draw near to you.

A Thousand Years

*But do not overlook this one fact, beloved,
that with the Lord one day is as a thousand
years, and a thousand years as one day.*

2 PETER 3:8

Patience is a virtue that many people desire but very few possess. Have you ever prayed for patience? If so, then you've probably had to stand in long lines at the grocery store, sit in traffic jams, or wait at the doctor's office. Why? Unfortunately, there are no shortcuts to learning patience. If we cooperate, we can learn patience by having to wait. If we don't cooperate, we just become more impatient. It is our choice. Impatience is especially prevalent among Americans. Other cultures seem to tolerate inconvenience and change with more ease. Our cultural efficiency and technology seem to feed into our impatient attitudes. We have become accustomed to having what we want when we want it.

Here's truth: God's timetable is not ours. With the Lord one day is like a thousand years and, conversely, a thousand years is like a day. Sometimes God seems slow.

He allowed the Israelites to take forty years to travel from Egypt to the promised land—a trip that should have taken eleven days! Other times God seems fast. In an instant Saul was struck down on the road to Damascus and was converted. Saul immediately became the apostle Paul. He turned 180 degrees—from persecuting Christians to converting people to Christianity!

Submit to God's timetable. His ways are always perfect. Purpose to learn patience in times of waiting. Learn to trust God more and believe that His ways are best. Realize that when He decides to act, things can happen in an instant. But when He seems slow to respond, it's for a reason. Continue to pray. Patiently wait for Him to show you the next step, and do not move until He does. God is sovereign and in control. Acknowledge and embrace that fact. You can trust Him!

Would you describe yourself as patient or impatient? What are some ways you could learn to trust God more in times of waiting?

Intimate Fellowship

Casting all your anxieties on him,
because he cares for you.

1 Peter 5:7

How do we respond when our world seems to be falling apart? Do we sit quietly before the Lord, pouring out our heart to Him? Do we yearn for Him to speak truth into our situation? That would be the wise response. Yet many times we avoid intimate fellowship just when we need it the most. Why?

If we are honest, we fear truly exposing our hearts to God. Vulnerability is difficult, especially when we're struggling. What if God speaks to us about an area of our life that needs changing? Although change may be God's will for us, we may not want to change. It is easier to blame others for the pain we are experiencing. We have become accustomed to playing the role of a victim instead of looking in the mirror. Our pride convinces us that if others would change, everything would be fine. So instead of spending time alone with the Lord, we turn up the radio or TV, hang out with friends. . .anything to stay distracted and cope the best we can.

Yet we have shut out the very One who longs to help us. We have closed the door on the One who knows us through and through. God knows your heart, even when you try to hide from Him. He is not fooled. He sees. He knows. He cares. Jesus yearns to comfort you. He is the most faithful friend you will ever have. He desires to give you strength to change for your own good. Turn off the distractions and turn your eyes upon Jesus. Don't be afraid of what He may say to your heart. It will be life-giving truth covered in love. Why wouldn't you want that?! Enjoy intimate fellowship with Jesus.

When life becomes overwhelming, do you tend to run toward God or away from Him? Why? Do you sense that there are areas of your life in which He wants to bring about therapeutic change? If so, be willing to allow Him access.

Drop the Stone

"Let him who is without sin among you
be the first to throw a stone at her."

JOHN 8:7

Many of us are familiar with the biblical story of the woman caught in adultery. The scribes and Pharisees brought the woman to Jesus and placed her in the midst of a crowd. Putting Jesus on the spot, they quoted the Law of Moses, which stated that adulterers were to be stoned. Jesus turned the tables back on them by saying, "Let him who is without sin among you be the first to throw a stone at her." One by one they left the scene until only Jesus was left standing with the woman. Jesus said, "Neither do I condemn you; go, and from now on sin no more" (John 8:11).

We hate being judged by others. We abhor having stones hurled at us when we mess up. So why are we so quick to throw stones at others? A judgmental attitude toward others does not negate our own guilt. We are just as guilty before a holy God. James 4:12 reminds us, "There is only one lawgiver and judge, he who is able to save and to destroy. But who are you to judge your neighbor?"

Would you say that you are a hypocrite? When you sin, do you want mercy and forgiveness? Yet when others sin, do you desire justice and punishment? Perhaps your sin appears small, whereas theirs seems more grievous. Sin is sin. Although Jesus has forgiven you, it comes naturally to judge others who are just like yourself. In the above passage, Jesus was the *only* one without sin. He was the *only* one who could have thrown the stone. Yet He chose to drop it. He chose forgiveness rather than condemnation. Since you have been forgiven, drop the stone and walk away.

Have you ever had condemning stones hurled at you by others? How did it feel? Is it easy for you to judge others? Is there a situation where Jesus is asking you to drop the stone? If so, ask Him to help you.

Drop the Stone Again

Night and day among the tombs and on the
mountains he was always crying out
and cutting himself with stones.

MARK 5:5

Throwing stones at others may be tempting, but many times we use stones to hurt ourselves. In Mark chapter 5, Jesus tells the story of a man tormented by an evil spirit. He screamed out and inflicted pain by cutting himself with stones. Today, cutting has seen a resurgence as young people react to deep-seated pain and anguish. Instead of lashing out at others, they lash out at themselves. They are tormented like the man Jesus encountered. They do not know how to handle the pain in their heart.

You may not be physically cutting yourself, but self-inflicted emotional and mental anguish is just as damaging. You can replay lies over and over in your head that say you are unloved, unforgiven, or unworthy. Pain is inflicted as you hurl these emotional stones at your heart. A downward spiral ensues as hopelessness gives way to despair. This is *not* God's will for you! Jesus loves you unconditionally. He forgives you always. You are worthy because you are a child of the King!

Jesus came to the demon-possessed man and had mercy on him. He drove out the evil spirit, and the man was restored to his right mind. Jesus has come to you. Whatever past mistakes, whatever regrets, whatever "demons" you are fighting. . .Jesus is there. Drop the stone into His hands. Turn to Jesus for healing and restoration. Receive the forgiveness that His death offers you. Embrace the kind of love that He demonstrated to you. "But God shows his love for us in that while we were still sinners, Christ died for us" (Romans 5:8). Jesus is not throwing stones at you, so stop throwing them at yourself. Drop the stone.

Do you tend to attack yourself? When are you the most vulnerable? What positive steps might you take to stop this vicious cycle? Believe God and not yourself: You are dearly loved. Ponder that truth over and over in your mind.

Power in Forgiveness

Having the eyes of your hearts enlightened, that you may know what is the hope to which he has called you, what are the riches of his glorious inheritance in the saints, and what is the immeasurable greatness of his power toward us who believe, according to the working of his great might that he worked in Christ when he raised him from the dead and seated him at the right hand in the heavenly places.

EPHESIANS 1:18–20

Sometimes forgiveness seems utterly impossible. Betrayal or false accusations by someone we love can be difficult to overcome. Abuse or neglect can leave lasting scars. When we have been wronged, we naturally want retaliation and revenge. Resentment, bitterness, and anger are normal human reactions to pain. However, when we allow these negative emotions to take root, they begin destroying us. Our heart becomes hard and calloused. Hate replaces love.

True forgiveness is impossible without God's power. Forgiveness does not negate an offense or excuse the transgression. Our pain is acknowledged, yet we refuse to get even or take revenge. Instead, by faith we release the offender to the Lord. "Beloved, never avenge yourselves, but leave it to the wrath of God, for it is written, 'Vengeance is mine, I will repay, says the Lord'" (Romans 12:19).

As Jesus was dying on the cross, He forgave the thief beside Him. Then Jesus experienced the power of the resurrection. You too can experience power as you lay all the wrongs, hurts, pain, insults, and abuse at the feet of Jesus in an act of obedience. The power of the indwelling Holy Spirit gives you the ability to do something that is impossible in your own strength—forgive. Over time, your heart will be transformed by God's power. Hope, peace, and love will replace bitterness, anger, and hatred. There is power in forgiveness.

Refusing to forgive someone only hurts you.
You can experience freedom and power when you
choose to forgive. Is there someone you've
had difficulty forgiving? Ask the Lord to
give you the power to forgive today.

Well Watered

*"Blessed is the man who trusts in the LORD,
whose trust is the LORD. He is like a tree planted by
water, that sends out its roots by the stream, and does
not fear when heat comes, for its leaves remain green,
and is not anxious in the year of drought,
for it does not cease to bear fruit."*

JEREMIAH 17:7–8

Gardeners know that watering plants in the early morning best prepares them for the sun's intense heat later in the day. In the same way, we need to prepare ourselves by being well watered spiritually *before* the furnace of life leaves us parched and dried up.

In Jeremiah 17:5–8 a shrub in the wilderness is contrasted with a green, fruitful plant by the water. The parched shrub represents the man who trusts in man. There is no life-sustaining nourishment for the soul because his heart has turned away from the Lord. Like a parched and withered plant in intensifying heat, those who depend solely upon themselves dry up when trials and hardships come. They are unfruitful.

But those who trust in the Lord experience a completely different result. Their spiritual roots tap into the life-giving source: Jesus Christ, the Living Water. They are like the plant by the water that sends its roots into the stream. They are continually nourished—even when plagued by heat and drought. Miraculously, they continue to bear spiritual fruit, even in the worst of conditions.

How can you be planted by the water? How should you keep well watered *before* the heat rises? Trust in the Lord, not yourself. Make church attendance a weekly habit. Get involved in a Bible study or small group. Study God's Word daily and pray consistently. As your roots tap into the Living Water, you will be preparing for seasons of drought. When the heat does come, you will have no need to fear but will remain fruitful and nourished.

When life heats up, in whom do you trust?
Do you typically feel well watered or parched?
What steps could you take today to better
prepare yourself for a season of drought?

Those Whom We Dismiss

"For the LORD sees not as man sees: man looks on the outward appearance, but the LORD looks on the heart."

1 SAMUEL 16:7

Whom might we dismiss as being unworthy to be used by God? We may erroneously believe that God could never use us. The truth is God can use anyone! In fact, many times He chooses the least likely, the weak, and those whom others dismiss. Consider David, the shepherd boy, anointed by the prophet Samuel as the next king of Israel. Everyone assumed that one of David's older brothers would be God's choice. Yet God had different plans.

Why does God use those whom the world often ignores? His power can be more evident in those who are weak because they rely upon His strength and not their own. "For consider your calling, brothers; not many of you were wise according to worldly standards, not many were powerful, not many were of noble birth. But God chose what is foolish in the world to shame the wise; God chose what is weak in the world to shame the strong;

God chose what is low and despised in the world, even things that are not, to bring to nothing things that are, so that no human being might boast in the presence of God" (1 Corinthians 1:26–29).

Remember: God looks at the heart. A heart that seeks after the Lord will be used by Him—regardless of human abilities, talents, outward appearance, or the opinions of others. God delights in making the weak strong. God specializes in manifesting His power in and through unlikely human choices. His power is made perfect in your weaknesses because He alone receives the glory. Do not dismiss others and do not dismiss yourself! Seek Him and others will see the strength of the Lord in you.

Have you ever written someone off? Ask God to give you His perspective to see others and yourself as He does. Look for ways to encourage the marginalized and forgotten. You never know whom God may choose for an important divine assignment!

Red Light, Green Light

"My sheep hear my voice, and I know them,
and they follow me."

JOHN 10:27

Red light, green light is a favorite children's racing game. As one child barks out orders, the other children immediately respond. Green light means "go"—run as fast as you can! Red light means "stop" dead in your tracks. If you accidentally run on "red light," you must start over. Intent listening and immediate obedience are required to win.

What if we applied "red light, green light" to our spiritual lives? The apostle Paul compares the Christian life to a race. In 1 Corinthians 9:24 he writes, "Do you not know that in a race all the runners run, but only one receives the prize? So run that you may obtain it." How do we run the race in order to win an imperishable wreath? We must listen and then obey. In John 10 Jesus describes Himself as the Good Shepherd. As His sheep, we can discern His voice. He speaks to us through His Word, the Bible. He also communicates through the still, small voice of the indwelling Holy Spirit. Other people or even nature can communicate His truth to our hearts. Are we listening intently?

Once you hear God's voice clearly, do you obey? Or do you stop when He wants you to step out in faith or go and run ahead when He wants you to wait for His leading? Listen intently. Obey wholeheartedly. It's black and white—clear cut—stop or go. There is no middle ground—no straddling the fence—no hedging your bets. You are either obeying the Lord or disobeying Him. How would the Lord evaluate your listening skills? How would He assess your heart for obedience?

Do you yearn for God to speak to you, or do you pretend not to hear Him so that you can go your own way? Would you say that you typically run ahead of the Lord or lag behind? Cultivate your listening skills. Obey when you know that God has clearly spoken to you.

Rest Secure

"The beloved of the LORD dwells in safety.
The High God surrounds him all day long,
and dwells between his shoulders."

DEUTERONOMY 33:12

Security is something we desire yet often find elusive. Why? We may trust in the things of this life; however, life remains uncertain. There are no guarantees. Financial security: How much money will be enough? Home security: Are there areas in my home that are vulnerable to intruders? Job security: Can I count on my present job for years to come?

As women, we also tend to rely upon our feelings and emotions, yet they can deceive us. Insecurity is the result of building our lives on shifting sand instead of a solid rock foundation. What if we based our security on spiritual truth rather than worldly inconsistencies or emotional volatility? What a difference we would experience!

True security is found only in Jesus Christ. He is the same today, tomorrow, and forever. He does not change like shifting shadows. Feeling insecure is a spiritual red flag indicating that you've put your hope or trust in someone or something other than Jesus—the financial markets, a spouse, children, job, etc. Regardless of what life throws your way, you can rest secure in the arms of Jesus. He gives stability in the storms and direction in the journey. When your feet are firmly on the Rock, you have an unmovable foundation. You are secure! He will never leave nor forsake you. Nothing can ever separate you from His love! "We have this as a sure and steadfast anchor of the soul, a hope that enters into the inner place behind the curtain, where Jesus has gone as a forerunner on our behalf" (Hebrews 6:19–20).

Do you feel secure? If not, ponder what you might be placing your trust in. Do you think it's possible to feel secure even when your world seems to be falling apart? How? Put your trust in the Lord alone for your security. Rest secure in His steadfast love for you.

Kicking against the Goads

"Saul, Saul, why are you persecuting me?
It is hard for you to kick against the goads."
ACTS 26:14

Saul, a zealous Jew, perceived Christians as the enemy. Little did he know that Jesus would confront him while he was on his way to Damascus to persecute believers. Saul was suddenly struck blind and asked why he was opposing Jesus. Although the word *goad* is not used much in today's vocabulary, it is a spiked stick used for driving cattle. So what is Jesus communicating to Saul, and perhaps to us?

Jesus gave Saul a wake-up call by pointing out that when Saul resisted Him, he was only hurting himself. Just as if he were kicking the sharp end of a goad over and over again. We might use the analogy of "banging our head against the wall." Why would anyone want to do that? It makes no sense at all! The Lord Jesus desired a personal relationship with Saul and had plans for his life, yet Saul pushed back. Although Saul ran in the opposite direction, Jesus pursued him and literally brought Saul to his knees. Saul then recognized Jesus and believed. His life was transformed by God's power, and he became the great apostle Paul.

What about you? Have you resisted Jesus by "kicking against the goads"? Why would you want to make life more difficult than it already is? God has great plans for your life that can only be fulfilled with His help. "And I am sure of this, that he who began a good work in you will bring it to completion at the day of Jesus Christ" (Philippians 1:6). Quit resisting. Run to Jesus, not away from Him. Return to the Shepherd and Overseer of your soul. Allow God to transform your life and give you the peace that you have been searching for.

Have you ever resisted the love of Jesus? Why? Even when you run from Him, He pursues a relationship with you. If you've been running, stop and turn around. Receive His embrace so that you will experience His peace.

Negative Results Require Positive Change

*If any of you lacks wisdom, let him ask God,
who gives generously to all without
reproach, and it will be given him.*

JAMES 1:5

Do you ever feel like you're constantly making the same mistakes in life over and over again? Poor choices regarding finances, relationships, or our vocation can become very discouraging. Contrary to popular belief, practice does not make perfect; practice makes permanent. It seems obvious that if something isn't working, we need to implement change. However, change is difficult, especially if we are entrenched in bad habits. Although we may acknowledge that change is needed, we may be at a loss for how to take that first step.

The Lord desires that you make positive change in your life instead of repeating the same old mistakes. Poor choices can be the result of following worldly rather than spiritual wisdom. Or you may be impulsive and act before thinking. Instead of trying to figure life out yourself, humble yourself and ask the One who holds all wisdom and knowledge. Read the Bible and start making choices that align your life with spiritual truth. Give God permission to expose areas in your life that need changing. Acknowledge that you need His power to help. In your own strength, failure will surely continue.

Today, allow the Lord to show you the first step. Then tomorrow, let Him show you what's next. Continue following His lead day by day. Change may be painful, hard, and slow. But transformation will occur as God changes you from the inside out. Positive change will be the result as bad habits are broken. May this verse serve as an encouragement: "And let us not grow weary of doing good, for in due season we will reap, if we do not give up" (Galatians 6:9).

Are there areas of your life that are continual challenges? Why do you feel like that's the case? Are you willing to cry out to the Lord for wisdom in pursuing positive changes? What do you sense might be the first step?

Thwarted Plans

*Then Job answered the Lord and said: "I know
that you can do all things, and that no
purpose of yours can be thwarted."*

Job 42:1–2

Those are powerful words uttered by Job. Do we believe
them? Do we believe that God can do all things? Do we
believe that His plans will prevail? This truth assures us
that no one can prevent, hinder, obstruct, or derail God's
plans. He will not allow it. His will *will* prevail. This is
great news: no plan of God's will be stopped by anyone
or anything. Ponder that profound truth for a moment.
Let it sink it. Turn it over in your mind. What conclusions
can you draw?

Job was a righteous man, yet encountered horrific
trials. He lost his children, livestock, and camels in a
single day. At the time, Job didn't realize that God was
permitting Satan to test him in order to prove his faith
genuine. Even through Job's adversity, God had been in
control. God's plans can never be thwarted by Satan.

Trials do not negate God's sovereignty. When you

encounter trials and testing, you may feel as if God has forgotten you. It may seem that God is no longer in control or that His plans have been altered. That is simply not true. Nothing can circumvent His will. God is allowing your circumstances, as difficult as they may be. But peace and strength can be yours in the midst of the storm. Just ask. Submit to God's plans. Trust that He is working and has a divine purpose that can never be thwarted. He will see you through! "And after you have suffered a little while, the God of all grace, who has called you to his eternal glory in Christ, will himself restore, confirm, strengthen, and establish you" (1 Peter 5:10).

What is your reaction when encountering storms in life? Do you feel abandoned by God? Do you feel as though He is no longer in control? Have you ever trusted God in the midst of a trial and experienced His peace and strength? Elaborate.

Empathy

For we do not have a high priest who is unable to sympathize with our weaknesses, but one who in every respect has been tempted as we are, yet without sin.

HEBREWS 4:15

Jill and Samantha sat together in the doctor's waiting room. Jill bemoaned, "I hate waiting in the doctor's office! They *always* run behind!" Samantha seemed unperturbed as she calmly read a book. As a nurse herself, Samantha understood what transpires beyond the waiting room: Some patients require longer visits—so more time is taken. Patients call in and need to be seen that day—so they are worked into the schedule. Doctors take calls from physicians to discuss complicated cases. As the doctors run behind schedule, nurses try to work efficiently with pleasant attitudes toward patients who are "tired of waiting!" Yes, nurses get it. They have empathy because they have been there.

Jesus has been there too! He gets it. Jesus, God's Son, came to earth in the form of a baby; He knows exactly what it's like to be human. He has experienced everything you will. That's why He understands and is able to sympathize with your weaknesses. He doesn't get impatient or angry. Jesus realizes that sometimes emotions trump logic. He remembers that the spirit is willing, but the flesh is weak. Temptations came to Jesus just as they come to you. The difference is that Jesus never succumbed to temptation by sinning. This is great news! Because He has been there and triumphed victoriously, you too can experience victory in times of weakness. "No temptation has overtaken you that is not common to man. God is faithful, and he will not let you be tempted beyond your ability, but with the temptation he will also provide the way of escape, that you may be able to endure it" (1 Corinthians 10:13).

What are some of your weaknesses? Don't try to hide them. Instead, bring them to Jesus. He understands. He empathizes. As you lean on Him, His strength is made perfect in your weakness. Jesus has given you victory!

Prepare for Storms While It's Sunny

Come now, you who say, "Today or tomorrow we will go into such and such a town and spend a year there and trade and make a profit"—yet you do not know what tomorrow will bring.

JAMES 4:13–14

Whether it's disaster drills at work or fire drills at school, everyone wants to be prepared for an emergency. Emergencies come upon us without warning. If we don't prepare ahead of time, it will be too late to prepare in the midst of the crisis. We must instinctively know how to respond correctly.

What if we viewed our spiritual lives with that same kind of readiness by preparing for life's storms while things are going well? Police officers are trained at police academies. Soldiers are drilled at boot camp. We need to be prepared spiritually *before* the storms of life come. We do not know when a loved one might die unexpectedly or we might be diagnosed with a debilitating disease.

When life takes our breath away, how do we react? If we are prepared, we will know what to do even if we're an emotional wreck. We have been trained. We are ready. We will be victorious.

How should you prepare for storms while enjoying sunny days? Be a part of a community of believers. Get involved in a church and small group, meeting with other Christians on a regular basis. When the storms of life assail you, they will be your prayer support. Read God's Word daily. Let spiritual truth penetrate your heart. The Holy Spirit will bring God's truth to mind in your darkest hours. Spend prayer time with the Lord. Then, when you are scared and frightened, you will instinctively run into His arms. Prepare today and you will respond correctly in the midst of the storm. You will be able to stand in the Lord's strength.

How are you preparing yourself spiritually today for the unexpected storms of tomorrow? Resist complacency when life is going well. Storms will come. Prepare yourself now for victory.

Thy Will vs. My Will

"Pray then like this: Our Father in heaven, hallowed be your name. Your kingdom come, your will be done, on earth as it is in heaven."

MATTHEW 6:9–10

When the disciples asked Jesus how to pray, He responded by teaching them the Lord's Prayer. Unfortunately, our familiarity may cause us to recite it by rote rather than to consider the meaning behind the words we utter. When we ask that God's will be done on earth, we proclaim our submission to His authority over our lives.

This is not something to declare nonchalantly or to take lightly. When we ask for God's will to be done, we submit to His will above our own. We acknowledge His sovereignty and goodness. We defer to His ways. We may not always understand, but we believe that He knows best. "For my thoughts are not your thoughts, neither are your ways my ways, declares the LORD. For as the heavens are higher than the earth, so are my ways higher than your ways and my thoughts than your thoughts" (Isaiah 55:8–9).

It's difficult to submit to God's will when you fear that the future may hold hardship. We would rather avoid pain at all cost. But as your relationship with Jesus grows deeper, you will learn to trust Him more and more. Know in your heart that His ways are best. Release your worst nightmare to Him. Be willing to take the road where He leads, even if it means walking through pain. It's not always easy, but His will is perfect. He will walk with you. Believe His promise: "And we know that for those who love God all things work together for good, for those who are called according to his purpose" (Romans 8:28).

In what areas are you reluctant to ask for God's will to be done? How can you grow in your relationship so that you are able to trust Him more? If you are in a difficult place right now, allow Jesus to hold you tight and see you through. He will never let you go!

Love Demonstrated

*But God shows his love for us in that while
we were still sinners, Christ died for us.*

ROMANS 5:8

How is love demonstrated? Author Gary Chapman contends that there are five love languages that communicate love: spending quality time together, giving gifts, speaking words of affirmation, bestowing physical touch, and doing acts of service. Simply saying "I love you" is not enough. Words can be cheap if not backed up with actions. God didn't just profess His love for us; He demonstrated it in the most sacrificial way. He sent His only Son to die on the cross for sinful man. God lavished His love on us when we were rebellious toward Him.

How should you reciprocate God's love? In John 14:15, Jesus says, "If you love me, you will keep my commandments." In other words, don't just say that you love God; do what He asks you to do. Read the Bible and obey it! Don't just pick out verses that suit you or are easy to obey. Follow Him in the hard areas of life too: "Do not be anxious about anything" (Philippians 4:6); "Love your enemies and pray for those who persecute you" (Matthew 5:44); "You shall not lie" (Leviticus 19:11). God doesn't want lip service. He sees your heart. He knows whether you truly love Him. He cannot be fooled.

The greatest commandment is this: "You shall love the Lord your God with *all* your heart and with *all* your soul and with *all* your mind" (Matthew 22:37, emphasis added). God doesn't want half of your love, but all of it. Put Him first in your life—above your family, children, spouse, job, home, and material possessions. Following the Lord should be your number one priority. This can be difficult. But consider this: God not only created you; He has redeemed your life and given you everything you need. Will you enthusiastically reciprocate His love through your actions? Love is indeed an action verb!

If you have embraced the love that God has demonstrated toward you by accepting His Son as your Savior, do you see any connection between His love and your obedience? Explain.

Extend Grace, Not Retaliation

*If your enemy is hungry, give him bread to eat,
and if he is thirsty, give him water to drink.*

PROVERBS 25:21

Tit for tat. As humans, we all understand that mind-set. When we've been wronged, we instinctively want justice to be served. We want retaliation and payback. The inflictor of pain should experience the same severity of pain that they have inflicted upon us. It makes total sense.

But many times God's ways are just the opposite of our own. When Jesus experienced rejection, He showed compassion. When He was hated, He demonstrated love. When He was beaten and spit upon, He did not utter a word. As followers of Christ, we are called to emulate Him. How in the world is that possible? There is no way we can humanly love our enemies or pray for those who persecute us! That's right—we alone cannot! But because Jesus did, we can!

The secret to following Christ is to allow Him to live not only "in you" but "through you." How is this lived out? When God requires you to do something that goes against your human nature, admit it. Say, "Lord, I cannot do this in my own strength. It is impossible. But I am asking that by Your power within me, You enable me to be obedient in this area." God is faithful. He *will* do it! Extend grace, not retaliation. Forgive instead of holding grudges. Love when rejected. Do it all by His strength at work within you! "Now to him who is able to do far more abundantly than all that we ask or think, according to the power at work within us, to him be glory in the church and in Christ Jesus throughout all generations, forever and ever. Amen" (Ephesians 3:20–21).

How do you respond when someone offends you?
Are you more apt to extend grace or retaliation?
Have you ever experienced God's power to help you
in humanly impossible situations? Describe.
If not, why not ask Him for help the next
time you need to forgive someone.

Inadequate

For God gave us a spirit not of fear but of power and love and self-control.

2 TIMOTHY 1:7

Feelings of inadequacy plague all of us from time to time, especially in Christian service. Comparing ourselves with others can leave us believing that we do not measure up. We feel like a failure. Fear of humiliation tempts us to throw in the towel and give up. We must remember: feelings are not facts. Often our emotions can become stumbling blocks, especially in spiritual matters.

Ignore voices that focus on your weaknesses and conclude that you are inadequate. God's voice would never whisper that to your heart! Other people, Satan, or even yourself may try to make you feel that you fall short. But if the Lord has called you to serve Him in some capacity, you are more than adequate in Him! God did not give you a spirit of timidity or fear, but of power. God's strength is made perfect in your weakness. Remember: God does not call the strong and capable. He calls the weak so that they will rely upon Him. He receives the glory when your strength and adequacy come from Him alone. "But he said to me, 'My grace is sufficient for you, for my power is made perfect in weakness.' Therefore I will boast all the more gladly of my weaknesses, so that the power of Christ may rest upon me" (2 Corinthians 12:9).

The next time you encounter feelings of inadequacy, decide whose voice you will listen to—others' or God's. Embrace truth, and listen to your heavenly Father's voice. You are dearly loved and fully adequate in Him. You are highly qualified because you have been called by the King of kings and Lord of lords! That is *always* enough. *Always* sufficient. *Always* more than adequate.

Have you ever struggled with feelings of inadequacy? If so, in what areas of life? Fear and faith cannot coexist. When we exercise faith to believe what God thinks about us, fear dissipates. How could you take a step of faith and leave fear behind?

Hiding from God

But God shows his love for us in that while
we were still sinners, Christ died for us.

Romans 5:8

In the beginning Adam and Eve enjoyed an intimate relationship with God in the Garden of Eden. They walked and talked together throughout the day. Then Satan appeared on the scene and utopia was shattered in an instant. Satan lied and deceived Eve into believing that she could be like God by eating the forbidden fruit. Both Adam and Eve succumbed to Satan's temptation and disobeyed God. Guilt and shame immediately enveloped them as they felt a great chasm separating them from God. This estrangement compelled them to hide. God sought and found Adam and Eve hiding in the garden. He then demonstrated His unconditional love by providing animal skins to cover their nakedness. This was the first animal sacrifice to cover sin. (See Genesis chapters 2 and 3.)

We still hide from God today for the same reason—we too have sinned and are separated from God. Our guilt compels us to conceal that sin and pretend it doesn't exist, so we attempt to hide. Yet think about it. Can we *really* hide from God? God is omniscient—He knows all. He knows when we sin. He knows where we are. We cannot hide from God any more than Adam and Eve could.

God seeks you out when you are hiding. He knows just where to look. He comes to you and covers your sin with the blood of Jesus. Regardless of your sin, God still loves you. He forgives you. He wants your relationship restored. Come out of hiding. Confess your sin. Repent and receive forgiveness. Enjoy sweet fellowship where you can walk and talk with Jesus in the garden of your heart.

Have you ever tried to hide from God? Were you successful? Do you believe that God loves you even when you are disobedient and rebellious? Is there some sin that you are trying to cover up? If so, confess it and receive forgiveness so that your relationship with God can be restored.

Fight or Flight

*Thus says the LORD, your Redeemer, the Holy One of
Israel: "I am the LORD your God, who teaches you
to profit, who leads you in the way you should
go. Oh that you had paid attention to my
commandments! Then your peace would have
been like a river, and your righteousness
like the waves of the sea."*

ISAIAH 48:17–18

The fight or flight response is a physiological response
to a perceived threat. It is a natural phenomenon. When
facing danger or an unexpected event, it seems we're
wired to either fight or flee. Some people instinctively
run toward trouble in order to intervene, while others
step back to assess the situation before reacting. Both
responses have merit.

When a loved one is in crisis, what would God have
us do? Do we intervene to help or sit back to allow them
to figure things out for themselves? How do we know
when to take action and when to be still? If we rush into
the situation without wisdom, we can find ourselves in

crisis too. Lifeguards and firefighters have lost their lives trying to save others.

Only the Lord can impart the wisdom needed in times of crisis. It's a moment-by-moment, situation-by-situation, day-by-day process. You must stay so connected to the Lord, so focused on Him, that you will know when and how to assist and when to sit back. Jesus is the ultimate rescuer—the only Savior. Your overriding role is to point others to Him. He will surely let you know if you are to be used as His hands and feet. If you are not sure—wait. Pray fervently for wisdom. Listen. May the Prince of Peace be your guide.

Are you wired for fight or flight? How do you know when to act and when to sit back? If this is an area you'd like to grow in, be still and listen to the Lord's wisdom. He will guide you in the way that you should go.

A Game Changer

Having the eyes of your hearts enlightened, that you
may know what is the hope to which he has called
you, what are the riches of his glorious inheritance in
the saints, and what is the immeasurable greatness
of his power toward us who believe, according to the
working of his great might that he worked in Christ
when he raised him from the dead and seated him
at his right hand in the heavenly places.

EPHESIANS 1:18–20

Although Jesus' disciples tried to remain faithful, many
times fear took over and they faltered. Even Peter denied
knowing Jesus. Yet after the resurrection, something dra-
matically changed. The disciples were bold and fearless in
the face of opposition. They were willing to die martyrs'
deaths. What was the game changer?

In the Gospel of John, chapters 14–16, Jesus has an
intimate conversation with His disciples. He reassures
them that although He will be leaving them, He will
send them a Counselor—the Holy Spirit. Jesus said,
"When the Spirit of truth comes, he will guide you into

all the truth, for he will not speak on his own authority, but whatever he hears he will speak" (John 16:13). The Holy Spirit would be Jesus' indwelling presence, giving them power and strength.

Immediately after Jesus' death, the disciples feared for their lives as they huddled behind locked doors in the upper room. Suddenly Jesus came and stood in their midst! He told them to wait in Jerusalem for the Holy Spirit. The Holy Spirit was poured out at Pentecost (see Acts 2). The disciples were changed. They boldly stood up to the Sanhedrin and proclaimed truth eloquently. No fear! As a Christ-follower, that same strength is yours because of the Holy Spirit living in you! Claim it. Walk in it! There is no limit to what God can do through you when you rely upon the Holy Spirit's help! Nothing is impossible with God!

Is your life characterized by fear or boldness?
Have you ever asked for the Holy Spirit's power at
a time when you felt powerless and afraid? Describe.

Look in the Mirror

But be doers of the word, and not hearers only, deceiving yourselves. For if anyone is a hearer of the word and not a doer, he is like a man who looks intently at his natural face in a mirror. For he looks at himself and goes away and at once forgets what he was like. But the one who looks into the perfect law, the law of liberty, and perseveres, being no hearer who forgets but a doer who acts, he will be blessed in his doing.

JAMES 1:22–25

Physical exercise is paramount to maintaining a well-conditioned body. Personal trainers encourage clients to look in the mirror while exercising in order to assess correct technique. Improper body alignment can be corrected immediately in order to lower the risk of injury. Optimal physical health can be achieved by avoiding pitfalls early.

The same is true for our spiritual health: spiritual exercise is necessary. We must look into the spiritual mirror of God's Word. Our hearts need to be measured against this plumb line of truth. If we are out of alignment, we need to repent immediately. Early spiritual correction can prevent painful injury later. First John 1:9–10 states, "If we confess our sins, he is faithful and just to forgive us our sins and to cleanse us from all unrighteousness. If we say we have not sinned, we make him a liar, and his word is not in us."

God's Word, the Bible, is a mirror into your soul. Do not ignore what God reveals. Do not pretend you are okay. If mirrors are useful to assess your physical condition, how much more is the mirror of God's Word essential to your spiritual health! Look in this mirror daily, and don't forget what you look like. Align your life with biblical truth. Be a doer of God's Word, and you will be blessed!

Have you cultivated the habit of reading God's Word? Has it ever corrected you? Ask God to reveal an area in your life that needs to be consistent with His Word. Then walk the talk.

Withholding Love

"Teacher, which is the great commandment in the Law?" And he said to him, "You shall love the Lord your God with all your heart and with all your soul and with all your mind. This is the great and first commandment. And a second is like it: You shall love your neighbor as yourself."

What if we could see others through the eyes of Jesus? Jesus believed that every single person was worth dying for. It's difficult for us just to be nice, but Jesus went to the cross and died in order to give eternal life to those who believe. We're not even willing to hold our tongues so that others might see Christ in us and come to know Him. How arrogant and prideful we are at times! We sit in the place of God—judging others and determining if they are worthy of our love and respect.

May this be our prayer: God, help us. Change our hearts. Give us spiritual eyes to see as You do. Help us not to judge others based on race, physical appearance, education, socioeconomic status, or religion. Everyone is made in Your image. Help us to embrace that truth and act accordingly toward those we come in contact with. Every person has worth. If You value them, Lord, then we should too! You command us to love one another, yet it does not come naturally. Show us how to love as You do. We have been called to be Your hands and feet in order to extend Your love to those who need it most. When we refuse to love our neighbor as ourselves, we have become a stumbling block that may prevent them from experiencing Your love. Help us, Lord, by changing our hearts of stone. May we never withhold the love that You have lavished upon us! Help us graciously extend it to others.

Have you ever withheld love from someone because you have judged them unworthy? Ask God to help you see others as He sees them. Extend grace and love to someone today by His strength.

Be Willing to Ask God

Oh, the depth of the riches and wisdom and knowledge of God! How unsearchable are his judgments and how inscrutable his ways!

ROMANS 11:33

We typically don't ask a question unless we're prepared for the answer. Patients may ask their doctor about a terminal prognosis after considering death as a possibility. A wife may confront an unfaithful spouse after contemplating divorce. When we are afraid of the answer, denial may be our coping mechanism. If we don't ask the question, we can pretend that everything is fine.

Are we willing to ask God hard questions in order to gain His wisdom? We may avoid asking God because we fear that His answer might be different from our own. So we keep our questions to ourselves and skip merrily down the road we have chosen. Occasionally we might wonder if the Lord would choose a different path, but we're afraid to ask. If we're honest, we don't want to know His answer because we want to continue on the course that we've charted.

74

Face facts: God's wisdom is infinitely greater than your own! "For my thoughts are not your thoughts, neither are your ways my ways, declares the LORD. For as the heavens are higher than the earth, so are my ways higher than your ways and my thoughts than your thoughts" (Isaiah 55:8–9). His wisdom is unfathomable! He really wants the best for you, not the worst! So be willing to ask God for wisdom: Is this the man You have chosen for me to marry? Should I take this new job and move across the country? Is it time to downsize and sell our home? God cares about every aspect of your life. You matter to Him! Seek His wisdom. Believe that His answers are best because they are always filtered through love.

Is there anything that you've been unwilling to ask God about for fear of His answer? You need God's wisdom today. May He grow your faith to believe that He can be trusted. Ask for wisdom, and allow Him to lead you.

Set the Captives Free

"The Spirit of the Lord is upon me, because he has anointed me to proclaim good news to the poor. He has sent me to proclaim liberty to the captives and recovering of sight to the blind, to set at liberty those who are oppressed, to proclaim the year of the Lord's favor."

LUKE 4:18–19

Imagine being in solitary confinement where utter darkness envelops you. Your soul cries out in anguish as you long to escape. Suddenly you hear someone at your cell door! The key turns in the lock as the door swings open! A voice calls, "Come out! I am giving you freedom!" Would you choose to stay in your prison cell because you've become accustomed to the darkness, or would you choose to embrace freedom?

Our reality may not be a prison cell, but we can be held captive in other ways. The expectations of others, job demands, the pursuit of money and pleasure can all serve as prisons. Jesus came to set captives free by giving them spiritual sight. Jesus came to set us free! He opens the door to our prison cell and beckons us to follow Him into the light of day. The unknown may be scary. There is always a price for freedom, but Jesus paid it for us when He died on the cross on our behalf. He gave up His life so that we could experience freedom!

Don't remain in jail because it has become familiar. Don't stay an oppressed captive! Embrace the freedom that you have been given. "So if the Son sets you free, you will be free indeed" (John 8:36). Once Jesus has set you free, don't reopen the cell door and reenter prison! Captives know pain, anguish, and emptiness. Jesus has a better plan for your life! Embrace it, and thank Him for the freedom that He has bought for you!

Have you ever experienced being held captive by something or someone? What steps could you take to walk in the freedom that Christ came to give you? Step out in faith today!

Dying

And he said to all, "If anyone would come after me, let him deny himself and take up his cross daily and follow me. For whoever would save his life will lose it, but whoever loses his life for my sake will save it."

LUKE 9:23–24

How would we react if we knew that today would be our last day on earth? What would be our priorities? Would we worry about paying bills or obsess about work deadlines? Probably not. Our focus may turn to the spiritual reality that soon we will see our heavenly Father and be ushered into heaven. Are we ready? Hopefully we have the assurance of eternal life because we have received Jesus by faith (see 1 John 5:11–13).

What if we could live today with a spiritual mindset? In Matthew 6:25–34, we are told not to worry about tomorrow. In Colossians 3:2 the apostle Paul encourages us, "Set your minds on things that are above, not on things that are on earth." How is that done when it's so easy to focus on earthly endeavors?

It's a paradox: If you hold on too tightly to this life,

you will lose it. Yet if you give up your life, you will save it. You must die to self in order to truly live. Dying to self means allowing Christ to live in and through you by following Him and being obedient to His Word. You will experience His presence and power in your life on a moment-by-moment basis. When you dwell in God's presence, the things of this world are put in their proper place because you will have spiritual eyes to "see" things as they truly are. Worldly problems appear trite and insignificant compared to the greatness of His glory! It is only in giving up this life that you will truly find life!

Read 1 Timothy 6:17–19. Would you say that you have taken hold of that which is truly life? Where is your focus? Ask the Lord to help you gain spiritual perspective while living in this world.

Trusting in the Pain

*Even though I walk through the valley of the shadow
of death, I will fear no evil, for you are with me;
your rod and your staff, they comfort me.*

PSALM 23:4

David knew what it was like to walk "through the valley of
the shadow of death." King Saul pursued David for four
years in an attempt to take his life. As David hid in the
caves of En Gedi, he trusted his Good Shepherd to guide
and protect him. In response to God's presence, David
chose faith over fear and in turn received God's peace.

The apostle Paul pleaded with the Lord three times
to have a "thorn. . .in the flesh" removed (2 Corinthians
12:7). Three times the answer was no. In response, Paul
wrote in 2 Corinthians 12:8–10, "Three times I pleaded
with the Lord about this, that it should leave me. But he
said to me, 'My grace is sufficient for you, for my power
is made perfect in weakness.' Therefore I will boast all
the more gladly of my weaknesses, so that the power of
Christ may rest upon me. For the sake of Christ, then, I am
content with weaknesses, insults, hardships, persecutions,

and calamities. For when I am weak, then I am strong."

You may not be running for your life like David or have a thorn like Paul, but you can suddenly find yourself in a painful valley. As pain pierces your soul and fear grips your heart, remember this: the same God who watched over David watches over you! He knows the valley you are in and the pain you are experiencing. God is walking right beside you! Allow your Good Shepherd to comfort you. He will fight your battles and draw you close for comfort. His presence can dissipate fear and worry. Trust Him, and receive His sufficient grace!

Have you ever had to walk through a deep valley?
What sustained you? If you are in one now,
meditate on Psalm 23. Trust your Good
Shepherd to comfort and uphold you.
Allow His presence to take away your fear.

Spiritual Glasses

That the God of our Lord Jesus Christ, the Father of glory, may give you the Spirit of wisdom and of revelation in the knowledge of him, having the eyes of your hearts enlightened, that you may know what is the hope to which he has called you.

EPHESIANS 1:17–18

As Louise awoke one morning, she experienced sudden vision loss in her left eye! After seeking medical help, she was diagnosed with NAION (non-arteritic anterior ischemic optic neuropathy). Although her right eye was still functioning, her overall vision had been severely compromised. Images seemed distorted and out of focus. Objects appeared blurred rather than clear. Physical blindness is one thing, but spiritual blindness is quite another.

All of us are born spiritually blind, unable to discern spiritual truth. Through faith alone, we can accept Jesus as our Savior and receive spiritual life. We are all sinners in need of a Savior. Jesus died on the cross to offer us forgiveness. When we receive Him by faith, we are born again—born spiritually. The eyes of our heart are opened.

It's as if we've been given spiritual glasses. We are able to understand the Bible for the first time. We view the world through God's lenses. Spiritual clarity becomes reality.

Yet even with the ability to understand spiritual truth, your spiritual glasses may become smudged from time to time. This happens when sin creeps into your life. Sin distorts God's truth and clouds your spiritual vision. What is the remedy? Read the Bible daily in order to discern if there is any sin attempting to get a foothold into your life. Confess it immediately so that your spiritual vision is restored. Strive with God's help to keep your spiritual lenses clean.

How would you assess your spiritual vision? Are you spiritually blind or has your vision become cloudy? How? The Lord has given you spiritual glasses to help you see the world as He does. Ask the Lord to help you recognize sin and confess it promptly so that your spiritual glasses will remain free of smudges.

Pain for the Sake of Love

Greater love has no one than this,
that someone lay down his life for his friends.

JOHN 15:13

The day started out somber, as clients and their invited guests gathered at the rehab facility. No one knew exactly what to expect, although everyone had been warned that the weekend would be emotionally intense. After several small group breakout sessions, the clients stood one by one and told their personal stories. Admitting that they were powerless over their addiction, they acknowledged the pain that they had brought not only to themselves but to their loved ones. Every heart in the room was moved upon hearing these poignant stories. Then each family member stood one by one behind the microphone. With their loved one facing them, they conveyed how their loved one's behavior had affected them. The pain was deep and emotions raw. The audience sat motionless as everyone absorbed the pain being recounted.

Yet amid a room full of pain and heartache, love prevailed. Each family member had taken the time to be present for their loved one that weekend to show their support. Despite the hurt, deception, pain, and lies, love overcame. They demonstrated unconditional love by simply showing up. That action spoke volumes. Love triumphed over the pain. Through the tears, love soothed hearts. Hope was birthed. A new day had dawned.

Many times when you lay down your life for others, it hurts because it costs you something. Whether it's your time, talent, or treasure, you are sacrificing something precious and giving it to them. Sometimes extending love means enduring pain. May Jesus inspire you: "But God shows his love for us in that while we were still sinners, Christ died for us" (Romans 5:8). Whenever unconditional love is expressed, love triumphs over pain. It is worth the price.

Jesus certainly knows about pain for the sake of love. How might you show unconditional love to someone? How might God be calling you to lay down your life for another? Ponder that thought. Then act upon God's nudging.

Gain God's Perspective

But when I thought how to understand this,
it seemed to me a wearisome task, until I went into
the sanctuary of God; then I discerned their end.

PSALM 73:16–17

Many circumstances in life seem perplexing or unfair. We try hard to sort out the facts and logically understand what is happening, but still fail to connect the dots. Perhaps we replay scenarios over and over in our minds hoping to arrive at different solutions. As humans, we lack perfect wisdom and understanding.

"If any of you lacks wisdom, let him ask God, who gives generously to all without reproach, and it will be given him" (James 1:5). Only God has the wisdom we desperately need. But unfortunately, prayer is not always our first response when life becomes confusing. Often we call a friend or spend countless hours trying to figure things out on our own. Frustration, weariness, and discouragement can set in as we go around and around in circles, getting nowhere. The psalmist expresses the same sentiment and admits to becoming weary in his quest for understanding. . .*until* he went into God's presence! Suddenly everything changed. His spiritual eyes were opened to see truth from God's perspective rather than his own.

Life seems unfair until you spend time with the Lord—and not just five minutes here or there. You have to "go into his sanctuary." You must draw close and stay awhile so that you are able to hear Him speak to your heart. Listening takes time. Yet when you dare to spend time with the Lord, you gain spiritual understanding and strength. God will reveal things to you in those quiet moments to bring clarity to your situation. Then He will use you to strengthen others with the spiritual truth you have gleaned in His sanctuary.

Does life often feel confusing? Where do you typically turn to gain understanding? The next time you desire wisdom, ask God. Open your Bible and be enlightened by spiritual truth. Spend time in prayer by pouring out your heart to Him. Then listen to the wisdom He imparts.

The Lord's Question

"You shall have no other gods before me."
EXODUS 20:3

Certain moments in life can steal your breath away. Suddenly being laid off work or receiving a cancer diagnosis feels like having the wind knocked out of you. When life surprisingly throws you a curveball, God may ask you a hard question: "Am I enough?" Circumstances can strip you of life's pleasures or stabilities. Even though you feel vulnerable and alone, that is not the case. God is right there beside you. You may not feel His presence, but He is there! Hard pressed as though you're being sifted through a sieve, you wonder whether anything will be left when it's over. Be assured, God will still be there. But here's the question: Is He enough?

A yes answer doesn't negate the pain and heartache you're going through. It doesn't mean you feign happiness and act like everything's fine. It means that deep down in your soul, you know that the Lord is for you. We acknowledge that He is with us because nothing can separate us from His love nor pluck us from His hand.

We have hope that He will lead us through this valley to the other side. As we cling to these truths, peace rules our heart, strength is ours for today, and hope lights our way for tomorrow.

If no is your answer, allow the Lord to examine your heart. An idol may have usurped God's rightful place. When you look to anything other than God for fulfillment, contentment, or joy, an idol has replaced God. Consider some potential idols: jobs, children, spouse, health, grandchildren, homes, pets—the list goes on and on. Prepare your heart now to answer that tough question. God is enough! He is all you ever need. He is your all in all!

Are there any other gods before the Lord in your life? What are they? Purpose to put the Lord first so that when your breath is taken away, He will enable you to stand. He is more than enough! Trust Him and see!

Remind One Another

Therefore I intend always to remind you of these qualities, though you know them and are established in the truth that you have.

2 PETER 1:12

Peter knew the importance of reminders—because people are forgetful. Even mature Christians sometimes forget how to swim when suddenly tossed in the deep end of life. They might even forget to yell for a life preserver! God did not intend for us to struggle alone. From time to time we need to be reminded of truth because our enemy is constantly whispering lies to our hearts. When we're most vulnerable, the lies come quicker, louder, and with greater intensity. During severe testing, forgetfulness seems to escalate with all of us.

Cultivate some intimate relationships where you can be real and vulnerable. In humility, share your struggles. Don't pretend that everything is fine. Storms are nothing to be ashamed of—they're part of life. In the midst of the storm, don't allow pride to get in your way. This may prevent someone from reminding you of truth. They might not even realize that you are drowning. Yell for a life preserver!

Thankfully, storms don't last forever! When your storm passes, you will then be in a position to encourage someone who may be heading into a storm themselves. "Blessed be the God and Father of our Lord Jesus Christ, the Father of mercies and God of all comfort, who comforts us in all our affliction, so that we may be able to comfort those who are in any affliction, with the comfort with which we ourselves are comforted by God" (2 Corinthians 1:3–4). Remind them of God's great love and mercy toward them. Remind them to keep their eyes on Jesus, not on their circumstances. Remember Peter? Look at Jesus, not the waves! We all need to be reminded of God's truth.

Do you have a close friend you can confide in? Or do you tend to keep to yourself when going through difficult times? Reach out and share your heart. Be there to remind someone of God's truth.

Asking for Help

Moses' father-in-law said to him, "What you are doing is not good. You and the people with you will certainly wear yourselves out, for the thing is too heavy for you. You are not able to do it alone."

EXODUS 18:17–18

Moses sat alone judging the Israelites from morning till evening day after day. Jethro, his father-in-law, could plainly see that Moses was exhausting himself. The task was too great for just one man. Moses desperately needed help, yet either he could not see his need or he did not want to ask for help. Jethro advised Moses to appoint trustworthy, God-fearing men who would be able to settle small matters. Moses listened and followed Jethro's wise counsel.

Asking for help is difficult for many of us. We would rather help someone else than to ask for their help. Why? Perhaps we don't want to be perceived as weak or needy. Maybe we like to be in control. The truth is we *are* needy and we are *not* in control! That's why Jesus exhorts us to ask Him for help. "Come to me, all who labor and are heavy laden, and I will give you rest" (Matthew 11:28).

Others may want to help you, but you may need to ask them. Have you ever considered that asking for another's help affirms their worth? It communicates your belief that they have something of value to offer you. You may not think that you are needy—and perhaps you're not. But independence prevents others from receiving the blessing of giving. Has anyone ever offered to help you do something? How did you respond? Don't deprive them of the opportunity to feel useful and needed. Accept their help graciously. Honor them. Bless them. Ask for help from someone today.

Would you rather help others or ask for help yourself? Why? What reasons prevent you from asking for help? Is there an area of your life where you need help? Identify it, and share your need with someone who is yearning to help you. Give them the blessing of feeling needed.

Don't Hold On to Heartache

He heals the brokenhearted
and binds up their wounds.

PSALM 147:3

Heartache and pain are familiar to all of us—whether it's because of situations, relationships, or failures. Do those painful memories define us? Pain can overshadow God's blessings if we refuse to let go and move forward. The half-empty glass becomes completely dry when we focus on what's lacking instead of God's grace in our lives.

Although Joseph's young life was marked by betrayal, hatred, and jealousy toward him, he refused to hold on to heartache (see Genesis 37–50). His brothers sold him into slavery where he was transported to Egypt. Then Joseph spent many years in prison after Potiphar's wife falsely accused him of rape. Although Pharaoh's chief cupbearer promised to remember Joseph after he was released from prison, he was forgotten. Joseph could have easily become angry, bitter, or depressed. Yet instead he chose to focus on God's perspective. Joseph forgave his brothers and was able to say to them, "As for you, you meant evil against me, but God meant it for good, to bring it about that many people should be kept alive, as they are today" (Genesis 50:20).

Tragedy occurs. Relationships are broken. Evil may seem to triumph. Yet the God of Joseph is still sovereign in your life today! God desires that you hold on to Him, not your heartaches. When you do, your perspective changes. Like Joseph, you can be assured that God is working all things together for your good (see Romans 8:28). Trust Him. Experience the peace of His presence. Inner joy is possible, even in the midst of tears. Allow Him to fill your cup to overflowing. Don't hold on to heartache—cling to Jesus instead.

Have you ever experienced rejection or betrayal? How did you react? Do you tend to hold on to heartache or trust God? If you are experiencing a painful situation now, turn to the Lord and lay your burden at His feet. Ask Him to heal your heart, bind up your wounds, and help you trust Him. May His peace flood your soul!

Pride Can Hinder Healing

Is anyone among you suffering? Let him pray. . . .
Is anyone among you sick? Let him call for the
elders of the church, and let them pray over him,
anointing him with oil in the name of the Lord.

JAMES 5:13–14

Being vulnerable and real is not easy. Impression management compels us to pretend that all is well. We share happy family pictures on Facebook of our daughter's wedding or our latest vacation. Little does anyone know that our own marriage is on the rocks and our daughter is battling anorexia. Life is spiraling out of control, yet we're afraid that friends would abandon us if they knew the truth. So we keep our struggles private and suffer alone. Pride may be hindering our healing.

Jesus often healed the sick and afflicted. Most of these miracles were performed publicly rather than privately. Jesus healed the hemorrhaging woman in a sea of people. The blind man at the pool of Siloam was given sight after Jesus put mud on his eyes. Friends had to lower a paralytic man through the roof to Jesus because of the crowded room. The underlying purpose of Jesus' miracles was to bring glory and honor to His heavenly Father.

What if God wants to heal you or a family member through intercessory prayer? How can others pray if they are unaware of your needs? Has pride prevented you from being honest? God calls us to pray for one another. Pick a few close friends you feel safe with. Share your heart. Ask for their prayers for healing or comfort. Feel your burden lifted as God intervenes and carries you. Life situations may not immediately change, but your inner spirit will be renewed with hope that comes from God through the intercession of His saints. The Lord will be glorified!

Are you terrified of being real for fear of abandonment by friends? Have you ever experienced healing or comfort through intercessory prayer? Please share. If you are struggling now, humble yourself with a close friend and ask for their prayers.

Immediately

Therefore, if anyone is in Christ, he is a new creation.
The old has passed away; behold, the new has come.

After Jesus was baptized by John the Baptist, He was led into the wilderness and tempted for forty days. Jesus victoriously defeated Satan and began His earthly ministry. In Mark 1 the word *immediately* is used nine times and *at once* is used as well. When Jesus came on the scene, things began to happen! *Immediately* Jesus entered a synagogue in Capernaum on the Sabbath and cast out a demon. *At once* his fame spread. *Immediately* he left the synagogue and learned that Simon's mother-in-law was sick with a fever, so Jesus healed her. When a leper approached Jesus and was touched by Him, *immediately* the leprosy left him.

Jesus began His earthly ministry in a whirlwind. He was a man of action who shook things up *immediately*! The world was never the same—and never will be. When we allow Jesus to come on the scene of our hearts and lives, we will never be the same. He will shake things up and change us forever. The Holy Spirit *immediately* resides within us and begins His work of transformation. We are new creations *immediately*!

Don't become discouraged if you don't notice instant results. Spiritual maturity takes time. Heart transformation is a process. But rest assured, Jesus is on the scene! Jesus will challenge you to leave your worldly nets, like the disciples, and follow Him. He will make you clean as He heals you from the inside out. Your sins are forgiven. Will you give Him access by opening the door of your heart? "Behold, I stand at the door and knock. If anyone hears my voice and opens the door, I will come in to him and eat with him, and he with me" (Revelation 3:20).

Have you become a new creation in Christ by accepting Jesus as your Savior? If not, what is preventing you from making this decision? Does discouragement over lack of spiritual growth concern you? Ask the Lord for help in areas where you'd like to see change.

Speaking Truth

Rather, speaking the truth in love, we are to grow up in every way into him who is the head, into Christ.

EPHESIANS 4:15

Communication can be tricky because two parties are involved—one speaks while the other one listens. Effective communication greatly depends on the condition of both people's hearts. If the speaker's heart conveys a judgmental or condemning attitude, the hearer immediately erects walls of defense. Words should be undergirded by love. On the other hand, if the listener's heart is hard, truth will not be received even if it's spoken in love. Hard hearts are as impenetrable as a brick wall.

So how should you speak truth to those who need to hear it? First, make sure that your heart is in the right place. What is your motivation? Are you trying to change them? Remember, that is God's place, not yours. You are called to love, even while speaking hard truth. If your heart is not where it needs to be, confess it. Ask God to fill your heart with His love so that it can overflow to others. Pray that your words are seasoned with truth and grace.

Once your heart is overflowing with love, be bold and speak truth. If the person is not open to hearing it, wait. The timing might be better later. Pray. Listen to the Lord's prompting. Don't give up. Ask God to till the soil of their heart to soften it. Wait for an open door. Only God can bring down brick walls. In the meantime, look for others with receptive hearts. Who has God brought into your life with a heart prepared to hear His message? May He give you eyes to see where to plant His seed of truth. Let love be your guide.

Is there someone in your life who has rebuffed your efforts to speak truth to them? Was love present in your heart? Describe times when the Lord has opened doors for you to speak truth into the life of another. How were you able to discern the right timing?

Act Now

Do not withhold good from those to whom it
is due, when it is in your power to do it.

PROVERBS 3:27

Kelley and Esther attended the same Bible study on Monday evenings. On one particular Monday, Kelley greeted Esther and asked how she was doing. Although Esther said, "Fine," her countenance revealed a different story. As Kelley inquired further, Esther poured out her heart. Kelley listened sympathetically. Esther was a public school teacher who yearned to make a difference. But each year the administration gave her the most undesirable class assignment. Esther had become downtrodden and discouraged. She was trying to discern whether to persevere in her current position or pursue other job opportunities.

After Bible study that evening, Kelley decided to pray for Esther. By faith she believed that God had a good plan for Esther. Kelley reached out to anyone she knew with connections to Christian schools. She prayed for open doors for Esther. In time, Esther landed a dream job where she could let her light for Jesus shine brightly—where her gifts and abilities would be appreciated instead of stymied. God had lifted her out of the pit and placed her in an environment where she could thrive for Him!

Have you ever considered that perhaps you may be the answer to someone else's prayer? God may want to use you in some way to bring about His will in another's life. Unfortunately, many times we are so focused on our own problems that we fail to see the needs of those around us. Ask the Lord for eyes to see and a heart to listen. When it is in your power to help someone, do so! We are the hands and feet of Jesus. We can also be His eyes and ears. May we have courage, boldness, and willingness to do something!

Do you readily "see" the needs of others, or do you tend to be too busy or preoccupied? Do you pray for their needs? Have you ever been used by God as an answer to someone else's prayer? Please describe.

Rule Followers

*"The Sabbath was made for man, not man for
the Sabbath. So the Son of Man is lord
even of the Sabbath."*

MARK 2:27–28

The Pharisees were rule followers. They prided themselves in knowing *and* following the law. In fact, they loved pointing fingers at those breaking the rules—even Jesus! One day as Jesus and His disciples were passing through the grain fields, the hungry disciples plucked some grain. The Pharisees became irate because harvesting was forbidden on the Sabbath. Jesus reminded them that even King David and his men entered the house of God and ate the bread of the Presence. Jesus set the record straight by clarifying that God made the Sabbath as a refreshment for man, not as another "rule" to keep. The Pharisees loved judging others because they were self-righteous. They mistakenly thought that if they kept the law, they were acceptable in God's sight and better than others. Pride and arrogance had blinded them spiritually and prevented them from embracing truth.

The Ten Commandments reflect God's perfect standards. They also reveal that we are sinful because no one can perfectly keep the law (see Romans 3:23). However, Jesus fulfilled the law that we can't keep and died in our place so that we could live in freedom. That does not mean that we are free to sin—just the opposite. We are free to live in the grace that Christ gives and follow Him.

Follow Jesus, not rules. Like the Pharisees, you have a choice. You can either follow rules or follow Jesus. When you choose to follow rules, pride creeps in. You can easily become puffed up and begin judging others. As legalism becomes your religion, joy disappears. A critical, judgmental attitude defines you. May your heart yearn to follow Jesus more than a list of rules. He *is* the Lord of the rules!

Do you tend to be a rule follower? Elaborate. Have you ever experienced a legalistic attitude in yourself or others? If so, did it draw others to Christ or repel them? Evaluate your own heart. Emphasize following Jesus over following rules.

Guess Who's Coming to Dinner?

"Behold, I stand at the door and knock. If anyone hears my voice and opens the door, I will come in to him and eat with him, and he with me."

REVELATION 3:20

The evening would be a night to remember. Delicious catered food displayed by efficient servers. Fifty people mingling and talking to one another. Worshipful music stirring hearts. Perfect weather. A moving PowerPoint presentation. The event at her home would be a smashing success and raise support for the ministry that she was so passionate about. Jenna could envision it!

Jenna was so excited as she went down her checklist: hire caterer; design, order, and mail invitations three weeks beforehand; print name tags; rent chairs; line up Christian musicians. Jenna's emotions were soaring, until the responses started coming in: "My daughter is getting married." "We're heading out of town." "I'm watching my grandchild." Jenna was reminded of the story in Luke 14 where a man gave a great banquet and invited many people. However, when it came time to attend the banquet, all the guests had excuses. "Will anyone come to my event?" Jenna wondered.

Jenna hated to admit it, but her emotions started to take a downward turn as disappointment set in. She wanted to share this ministry with others so that they could catch the vision of what God was doing. It was then that the Lord quietly whispered, "I'm coming!" Wow! The King of kings and Lord of lords had responded "Yes"! That was all the encouragement Jenna needed. Jesus was coming to dinner! His presence alone would make it a success. It truly would be a night to remember! Jesus never refuses an invitation. He always responds "Yes." Invite Jesus to dinner. He is knocking at your heart's door.

Have you ever been discouraged by similar circumstances? How did you handle it? People can let us down—just like we can let them down. However, Jesus never fails us. Ask Jesus to dinner and share your heart with Him. He is never too busy. His response is always "Yes"!

Be Quiet So God Can Speak

Know this, my beloved brothers: let every person
be quick to hear, slow to speak, slow to anger.

JAMES 1:19

Have you ever been around someone who talks incessantly? It can be so exhausting that after a while you tune them out. Words can be powerful, yet verbosity is draining. We as parents yearn to impart truth and wisdom to our children. Yet in doing so, many times we feel as though our words ricochet off the walls. If our children are not open to receiving our message, we simply talk louder and longer by transitioning into lecture mode. Yet that doesn't seem to improve their listening skills one bit!

Have you ever pondered this thought: If we are talking so much, can our children hear the quiet, still voice of God speaking to their hearts? Sometimes we need to zip our mouths shut—even if what we have to say is wise and beneficial. Too much talking becomes a sensory overload—and others tune us out! Perhaps that's why many times God compels us to listen by whispering. In the quietness of your heart the Holy Spirit speaks when your heart yearns to listen. Let's face it, God's wisdom is far greater than our own!

If your tendency is to talk to your child until you're blue in the face, try listening more. Give God the opportunity to speak to them instead of you. Be quiet. In doing so, you will demonstrate your trust in God, not in your ability to convince them of anything. God is sovereign. He loves your children even more than you do. Give Him the chance to speak by being quiet. When you do speak, choose your words wisely so that they can be impactful and not ignored.

How are your words received by others? If you have children, have they ever tuned you out? Why do you suppose this happens? Try listening more and speaking less. Ask the Lord to show you other action steps that you can take to help you communicate more effectively.

Be Ready

But in your hearts honor Christ the Lord as holy, always being prepared to make a defense to anyone who asks you for a reason for the hope that is in you; yet do it with gentleness and respect.

1 PETER 3:15

Emma was thinking "comfort" as she slipped on the gray cotton T-shirt before heading out the door to run errands. Standing in line at the post office, she allowed her mind to drift. An older gentleman behind her startled her by asking, "Who redeemed you?" She had no idea what he was talking about. *What a random question*, she thought. Then Emma remembered that the front of her comfy T-shirt said, *Forever Redeemed*. She smiled at the man and replied, "Jesus Christ!"

A young man covered with tattoos piped up and exuberantly exclaimed, "Me too!" He began giving testimony about how the Lord Jesus had transformed his life. Emma and this fellow Christian began sharing about the grace and love of Jesus while the older gentleman listened. As Emma was leaving the post office, even the postal worker exclaimed, "I like your shirt!"

You never know what divine appointments the Lord has lined up for you on any particular day. Who knew that a comfy T-shirt could evoke a lively discussion about Jesus with complete strangers? People are observing how you live your life. Be ready! Be prepared! These opportunities usually present themselves when you least expect it. Be attuned to the Lord throughout the day so that you will be able to respond to anyone with spiritual questions. Eternal seeds are planted when you give the reason for the hope within you. Sow His seed. Be used to spread the Good News of Jesus—our Redeemer!

Is it easy or difficult for you to talk to others about Jesus? Are you more comfortable sharing with friends or strangers? Ask the Lord to prepare you for the next time a situation arises so that you can be a bold witness to someone in need of Jesus. Be ready!

Whatever Is True

Finally, brothers, whatever is true, whatever is honorable, whatever is just, whatever is pure, whatever is lovely, whatever is commendable, if there is any excellence, if there is anything worthy of praise, think about these things.

PHILIPPIANS 4:8

We have a choice about what we allow our minds to dwell on. A wise woman once said, "We aren't responsible for the birds that buzz our heads, but we are responsible if we allow them to build a nest." Random thoughts may pop into our heads, but we must choose whether to dismiss them or to think about them. What criteria should we use in making that choice?

As Christians, we have an enemy—Satan, the father of lies. He attempts to deceive us just like he deceived Adam and Eve in the garden. Satan tempted Jesus in the wilderness by misquoting scripture. His tactics haven't changed. Satan speaks to us in lies or half-truths. If we take his bait, we start dwelling on them. Slowly we are led away from God as the downward spiral begins. How do we recognize his lies? How do we know when a thought is from our enemy? The apostle Paul urges us to "take every thought captive to obey Christ" (2 Corinthians 10:5).

Philippians 4:8 encourages us to think about "whatever is true." Truth is found in God's Word. It is the plumb line by which everything else is measured. That's why it's important to read and study the Bible. You are more adept at recognizing Satan's lies if God's truth is written on your heart. You need to think and meditate on truth, not lies. When truthful thoughts flood your mind, you are drawn closer to Jesus. You will experience His peace. The choice is yours. What will you choose to think about?

When you examine your thought life, what are you most likely to think about? Is it true, false, or indifferent? Do you have difficulty recognizing lies from Satan? What steps can you take that would help you think about "whatever is true"?

Would You Dare?

*"No one can serve two masters, for either he will
hate the one and love the other, or he will be
devoted to the one and despise the other.
You cannot serve God and money."*

MATTHEW 6:24

Emily grew up in a Christian home and asked Jesus to be her personal Lord and Savior at fifteen years old. Although she was a typical teenager in many ways, her heart desired to follow Jesus. During her college years she attended church and Bible study. Emily wanted to grow in her Christian faith. She wanted to live her life according to God's plan, not as the world dictated. She later married, had children, and started a career.

As Emily matured both physically and spiritually, she and her husband started experiencing financial success. Although the money was a blessing, she observed that some of their Christian friends had pulled back from the Lord in order to pursue worldly pleasures. As materialism grabbed their hearts, godly pursuits were left behind. Emily wondered if they might be tempted to do the same. So one day she prayed, "Lord, please do not bless us financially if it would mean that I would ever turn away from you."

Some people believe that money can buy happiness. God's Word is clear that your heart has to choose between the two. Either money has you or God has you. Nowhere in the Bible does it say that having money is evil. First Timothy 6:9–10 says this: "But those who desire to be rich fall into temptation. . . . For the love of money is a root of all kinds of evils." Would you dare pray as Emily did? Or would you desire material riches regardless of the cost? You must choose which master you will serve. You cannot serve both.

Are you content with the financial resources God has blessed you with? Or do you yearn to have more? What is your heart's treasure? If you would like to grow in this area, ask for the Lord's help. Ask Him for contentment and a heart that pursues Him.

Clothed in Righteousness

*I will greatly rejoice in the LORD; my soul shall
exult in my God, for he has clothed me with
the garments of salvation; he has covered
me with the robe of righteousness.*

ISAIAH 61:10

Olivia sat, arms folded across her chest, with her mind made up. No one was going to talk her out of it—not her counselor, her friends, or her parents. She had decided to start living with her boyfriend. "I'm eighteen and can make my own decisions," she reasoned. Olivia wore her boyfriend's jacket as a statement of defiance.

If our physical clothes can make a statement, what do our spiritual clothes communicate? Regardless of how much we spend on our wardrobe, we all wear polluted spiritual garments. Although we may want to wear a beautiful robe, we don filthy rags instead. Isaiah 64:6 states, "We have all become like one who is unclean, and all our righteous deeds are like a polluted garment." Our spiritual wardrobe seemed hopeless until God intervened! He purchased and gave us a garment of salvation, a robe of righteousness. This robe was bought through the death of His Son, Jesus. When we accept Jesus as our personal Savior, God puts Christ's righteousness on us. We wear His beautiful robe—a statement of His love!

As a Christian, you are adorned with an outer garment more beautiful than the most expensive article of clothing in the world! This robe never wears out or goes out of style. It is priceless and eternal. Clothes make a statement. What statement do you want to make to a watching world? Have you traded your polluted garment for a garment of salvation? If not, receive Jesus' robe of righteousness today and become a child of the King!

Have you given much thought to your spiritual wardrobe? Are you still wearing filthy garments, or have you accepted Jesus' robe of righteousness— purchased by God for you? All you have to do is accept it by faith. You are a beautiful child of God! Thank Him for His priceless gift.

God's Eyes

For the eyes of the LORD run to and fro throughout the whole earth, to give strong support to those whose heart is blameless toward him.

2 CHRONICLES 16:9

The lyrics of a children's Sunday school song of yesteryear warn us to be careful what we see, hear, and do. Not only do our daily choices have great impact, but our heavenly Father sees everything. Nothing escapes His notice as He looks down to earth with love.

Soon after creation, men's wickedness increased. God was so grieved that He regretted making man and planned to destroy His creation. But as He surveyed the earth, He saw one righteous, blameless man named Noah. God sent a flood but saved Noah and his family in an ark that Noah built following God's specific instructions (see Genesis 6). After the flood, man's heart still did not change. But God saw Abraham and decided to make him a great nation—one that would bless the whole earth through the coming of the Messiah. Abraham left his home and family to follow God, even though he did not know where he was going. "And he [Abraham] believed the LORD, and he counted it to him as righteousness" (Genesis 15:6).

What do God's eyes see when He looks down upon your neighborhood, your home, your heart? He is continually looking for hearts that are blameless toward Him. What does this mean? God knows that you will never be sinless. He is yearning for you to follow Him, rely upon Him, trust Him. When you seek Him, He gives you *strong support*. Imagine receiving power and strength from the Creator of the universe! May your actions and attitudes demonstrate your love of God. May He be pleased when His eyes see your heart.

Are you aware of God's watchful eye? How does that make you feel and why? Ask the Lord to give you the strength to walk in a manner that is pleasing to Him. Desire to follow His will for your life and to apply His truth.

Tangled in the Thorns

As for what was sown among thorns, this is the one who hears the word, but the cares of the world and the deceitfulness of riches choke the word, and it proves unfruitful.

Jesus often spoke to crowds using parables, illustrating spiritual truth through earthly examples that people could understand. The parable of the sower is a familiar one. The farmer sowed seed on four types of soil: the path, rocky ground, thorns, and good soil. The seed represents spiritual truth and the soil depicts the human heart. The seed's productiveness was dependent upon the condition of the soil (heart). The good soil was the most productive and fruitful.

We want our hearts to be good soil where God's truth can flourish and grow. As Christians, we hope that our lives are characterized by spiritual productivity and fruitfulness. However, we live in a thorny world with many cares and distractions. It is easy to become tangled in the thorns.

You can use your time, talent, and resources to pursue

spiritual or worldly gain. Be careful. Worldly riches can choke spiritual fruit. For example, pursuing financial success may rob you of time spent reading God's Word or attending church. Material wealth offers more opportunity for leisure and worldly pursuits. Maybe that is why Jesus warns in Matthew 19:23–24, "Truly, I say to you, only with difficulty will a rich person enter the kingdom of heaven. Again I tell you, it is easier for a camel to go through the eye of a needle than for a rich person to enter the kingdom of God." Riches are not sinful unless they become a stumbling block to spiritual growth. Do not allow riches or the cares of this world to choke out what God has planted. May your life be characterized by spiritual fruitfulness.

How would you evaluate your spiritual fruit—unproductive or a bumper crop? Ask the Lord to show you any worldly thorns that may be preventing spiritual growth. What changes might He be asking you to make in order to become more fruitful?

People Need the Lord

Humble yourselves, therefore, under the mighty
hand of God so that at the proper time he may
exalt you, casting all your anxieties on
him, because he cares for you.

1 PETER 5:6–7

Years ago Steve Green penned a song titled "People Need the Lord." Although we all need the Lord, not everyone acknowledges their need. Instead of turning to the only One who can truly help, they attempt to handle life on their own. It isn't until they are at the end of broken dreams that they call out to God for help.

Why does God allow trials to come into our lives or the lives of our loved ones? Many times the storms of life serve to get our attention so that we recognize our desperate need of God. He waits with open arms and a compassionate heart for us to cry out to Him. He wants to rescue, restore, and reassure. God will never leave nor forsake us—regardless of our circumstances or how we got there.

You may be quick to respond to the needs of your

family. You comfort and console by rushing to their aid—it feels good to be needed. But what if your help isn't helping? What if your help is preventing them from crying out to God? There is only one Savior, and it's not you. Divine help trumps your help any day. The next time someone turns to you for help, pray for God's wisdom. Ask the Lord how, if at all, you are to intervene. Above all, point them to Jesus, the One they truly need. People need the Lord. Be an ambassador for Christ and point others to the Savior!

Do you tend to be a rescuer and enabler? Do you think this has prevented someone from turning to God for help? Ask for God's wisdom in knowing when to intervene and when to sit back. Your help is good, but God is the One they need above all else.

Taste and See

Oh, taste and see that the LORD is good!
Blessed is the man who takes refuge in him!

PSALM 34:8

Enjoying a meal means savoring every bite! Chewing food slowly releases different flavors that are appreciated by our taste buds. Unique food textures can be distinguished. Chewing slowly enables enzymes to break down food for proper digestion. When we eat in a hurry, not only can indigestion occur, but we miss the taste and enjoyment that food was meant to give.

While physical food is pleasurable to our senses, it only holds temporary enjoyment. Spiritual food offers eternal satisfaction. What is spiritual food? Spiritual food consists of God's truth that nourishes our spirit. It brings hope, healing, direction, wisdom, and strength to our souls. It sustains us. How do we obtain this spiritual food? Open the Bible, God's Word. Read and meditate upon it. Obey it. Pray and pour out your heart to God. Listen for His still, small voice and follow His counsel.

Are you gulping down spiritual food in a hurry, or

are you savoring every bite? If you rush through reading the Bible or praying, you miss out on truly "tasting" the Lord. Just as your body uses physical food for energy, spiritual food infuses your spiritual life with strength and power. Spiritual food needs to be not only eaten but applied in your life. When time with the Lord is savored, you will not only "taste" spiritual food—you will be able to use it. His strength and power will be at work within you. "For this I toil, struggling with all his energy that he powerfully works within me" (Colossians 1:29). You will then "see" that the Lord is good! "How sweet are your words to my taste, sweeter than honey to my mouth!" (Psalm 119:103). Lord, may it be so!

Have you ever considered your need for spiritual nourishment? How do you obtain spiritual food? Ask the Lord to help you slow down so that you can savor every minute spent in prayer and in His Word.

Treasures Revealed

"Do not lay up for yourselves treasures on earth, where moth and rust destroy and where thieves break in and steal, but lay up for yourselves treasures in heaven, where neither moth nor rust destroys and where thieves do not break in and steal. For where your treasure is, there your heart will be also."

MATTHEW 6:19–21

Arlie and Myrtle were both moving to an assisted living facility. Downsizing required getting rid of earthly possessions that each had spent a lifetime accumulating. Letting go was difficult and painful. As items were boxed to give away, Myrtle lamented to her son, "You're taking away my life!" Arlie, however, approached her move quite differently. Her new room, which she would share with a complete stranger, had but one dresser and a single bed. Her granddaughter wheeled Arlie into her room for the first time and pointed out the window. Looking at the courtyard beyond, Arlie exclaimed, "What more could I need?"

Why the two completely different reactions to the

same scenario? Material possessions were important to Myrtle. She had become very attached to her treasures, so parting with them was painful. While Arlie had also enjoyed the finer things in life, she had learned to hold them loosely. So at the end of her life, Arlie was better able to focus on eternity as she let go of earthly treasures.

God wants you to enjoy what He gives you on this earth. Yet you need to recognize that this is not your home. Everything that you can see and touch is temporary. Someday you will have to let go, whether you want to or not. So learn to hold earthly treasures loosely now. Concentrate on treasures that will last forever—your relationship with the Lord and the advancement of His kingdom.

Do you tend to be a pack rat and have difficulty letting go of earthly possessions? Evaluate your heart. Where do your treasures lie—in things on earth or in heaven? True treasures are spiritual in nature. How could you concentrate more on heavenly rather than earthly treasures?

Me or You?

Let each of you look not only to his own interests,
but also to the interests of others.

PHILIPPIANS 2:4

What is your typical mind-set? Are you outward-focused, looking for ways to help others? Or do you tend to be inward-focused, thinking that the world revolves around meeting your needs? It is a difficult balance to maintain. This verse in Philippians acknowledges that we do need to care for ourselves, but not to the exclusion of others.

Where was Jesus' focus—on Himself or others? Jesus consistently set aside His own needs for the sake of other people. When He was physically exhausted, He took time to speak to the multitudes. Jesus stopped what He was doing to heal the sick. He demonstrated servanthood to His disciples by washing their feet. From a human perspective, He did not want to face crucifixion. Yet He chose to meet our needs first by making the ultimate sacrifice. Jesus gave His life so that we could live eternally.

As a Christian, you are gradually being transformed into the image of Christ by the Holy Spirit. This means that you begin to cultivate His attitude of servanthood. You are called to serve others for His sake. This requires sacrifice and self-denial. It's difficult, but not impossible. As you continue to grow spiritually, your heart is transformed and you are changed from the inside out. More of Jesus' character begins to manifest itself in your daily life. You will discover that meeting others' needs brings indescribable joy because you are walking in the footsteps of Jesus! There is a balance. You must keep yourself physically, emotionally, and spiritually strong so that God can use you. Meet your own needs, not for the sake of focusing on self, but so that you can optimally serve others.

Describe your typical mind-set. What are some ways that you might serve others? If you tend to help others to the exclusion of having your own needs met, what are some changes you might make? Consider that you will be most helpful when your own tank is full.

Idols Never Satisfy

*"You shall not make for yourself a carved image,
or any likeness of anything that is in heaven above,
or that is in the earth beneath, or that is in the water
under the earth. You shall not bow down to them
or serve them, for I the LORD your
God am a jealous God."*

EXODUS 20:4–5

The Ten Commandments were given to Moses by God on Mt. Sinai. The law is God's instructions for how to live life His way—the best way. The first four commandments refer to our relationship with Holy God, and the last six focus on our relationship with one another. Our need for a Savior is made apparent by our inability to keep the law: our sin has separated us from God. Jesus fulfilled the requirements of the law and took our punishment (death) so that we could be made righteous by faith.

When we accept Jesus by faith, the law does not become null and void. The second commandment is still applicable today. In the absence of carved images or a golden calf, we may erroneously assume that we don't worship idols. However, our subtle idols are just as deadly to our spiritual walk. In fact, throwing away a wooden statue may be easier than walking away from attitudes or material possessions that have captured our hearts.

Have any idols crept into your life and gotten in the way of worshipping God first? Material possessions, the pursuit of pleasure, or physical beauty can take on great importance. As you become overly focused on these, your time, energy, and resources are spent on them. Even family and friends may hinder us from loving God foremost. If something or someone trumps your love of God, it should raise a red flag. Only God can truly satisfy your soul. Obey this commandment by getting rid of any idols.

Are there any idols that have crept into your life and usurped God's rightful place? What are they? Read and meditate on Matthew 6:33. What action steps do you need to take to seek God first?

How Green Is My Valley?

The Lord is my shepherd; I shall not want. He makes me lie down in green pastures. He leads me beside still waters. He restores my soul. He leads me in paths of righteousness for his name's sake. Even though I walk through the valley of the shadow of death, I will fear no evil, for you are with me; your rod and your staff, they comfort me.

Psalm 23:1–4

Life consists of hills and valleys. We prefer the hilltops, but unfortunately, they don't last forever. Do we view valleys with disdain, dread, and fear? Valleys are difficult, yet they need not overtake us. Although the apostle Paul had experienced shipwreck, beatings, and imprisonment, he wrote, "We are afflicted in every way, but not crushed; perplexed, but not driven to despair; persecuted, but not forsaken; struck down, but not destroyed; always carrying in the body the death of Jesus, so that the life of Jesus may also be manifested in our bodies" (2 Corinthians 4:8–10).

Like Paul, we can experience hope and peace because of Jesus, our Good Shepherd. Even in the valleys, He provides green pastures. Ponder physical valleys. Because they are situated between hills, rainwater is funneled to the bottom. The grass is greener and trees provide shade from the scorching heat. Many times rivers flow through valleys, bringing water to sustain plants and animals.

When Jesus allows you to walk through valleys, He is always with you. He leads and sustains you. Jesus provides for you. He can bring hope, peace, and restoration in the valleys of life. The secret is not to panic but to rest in Him alone. Drink from the Living Water. Rest in the green pastures that He provides. You need not fear evil. Jesus is your comforter and protector.

Have you ever encountered a deep valley in life? Describe it. How did you handle it? Have you ever experienced God's presence in a valley? Ask the Lord to help you trust Him in the valleys of life. Look to Him to provide all that you need.

The Mental Game

For those who live according to the flesh set their
minds on the things of the flesh, but those who live
according to the Spirit set their minds on the things
of the Spirit. For to set the mind on the flesh is death,
but to set the mind on the Spirit is life and peace.

ROMANS 8:5–6

It has been said that golf is a game of six inches—referring to the distance between your ears. In other words, golf is a mental game. Mental toughness is imperative, and mental focus is crucial. Dwelling on bad shots is the kiss of death. Golfers must dismiss errant shots to focus on their current swing.

What about our mental spiritual game? Are we so focused on the negatives that we're oblivious to the blessings in our lives? The apostle Paul encourages us to "set our minds" on things of the Spirit rather than things of the flesh. Things of the Spirit are invisible, eternal, heavenly, and immutable, whereas things of the flesh are visible, temporary, earthly, and unstable.

Being "in the world but not of the world," you are

challenged to live on earth with a spiritual mind-set. Mental toughness and discipline are required to gain this perspective. "Take every thought captive to obey Christ" (2 Corinthians 10:5). Read the Bible often to focus on spiritual things and renew your mind. "Do not be conformed to this world, but be transformed by the renewal of your mind, that by testing you may discern what is the will of God, what is good and acceptable and perfect" (Romans 12:2). Joy will emerge. Peace will resonate in your soul. As you set your mind on God, He will open your spiritual eyes to see rainbows in the midst of life's storms and roses blooming among thorns.

How would you assess your mental spiritual game? Do you tend to set your mind on things of the Spirit or the flesh? How could you shift to a more spiritual focus? Ask the Lord for help so that life and peace will be yours.

Pray without Ceasing

Pray without ceasing.
1 Thessalonians 5:17

"Pray without ceasing." What a small yet powerful verse! Never stop praying, even if prayers have yet to be answered. That is difficult to do! God hears our prayers and answers them according to His will, not ours. He has three answers: yes, no, or not now. Times of waiting can lead to discouragement, so we may cease praying rather than pray without ceasing!

Prayer is conducting spiritual battle. It is hard and relentless, yet we must persevere in order to be victorious! Satan wins when we believe his lies—"The situation will never get better," "People will never change," "All hope is gone." If Satan convinces us that God is unable to intervene or that God doesn't love us, we may give up hope and stop praying. God's ways and His timing are usually not our own. Trust Him by believing that He knows best. Wait upon the Lord patiently. His arm is not too short. "For nothing will be impossible with God" (Luke 1:37).

Focus on the truth found in God's Word. Second

Corinthians 10:4 reminds us that "the weapons of our warfare are not of the flesh but have divine power to destroy strongholds." Prayer is that weapon because it unleashes God's power. Satan has been defeated, and he knows it. God is still on the throne, but Satan attempts to convince you otherwise. God can divinely intervene at any time and bring beauty from ashes. Believe God. Pray! "The prayer of a righteous person has great power as it is working" (James 5:16). Never give up hope. Never give in to Satan. You can have spiritual victory when you pray. So pray without ceasing, and believe God's truth, not Satan's lies!

Describe a time when you stopped praying for something or someone in particular. What made you stop? Have you ever experienced unexpected answers to your prayers? How did that affect your faith and prayer life? Is there an area in your life where you desire victory? Continue to pray, watch, and wait for God's answer.

God's Faithfulness

The steadfast love of the LORD never ceases; his mercies never come to an end; they are new every morning; great is your faithfulness. "The LORD is my portion," says my soul, "therefore I will hope in him."

LAMENTATIONS 3:22–24

Olivia had become so crippled by fear that she was unable to pray. Carly, her daughter, had run away three months ago and she hadn't heard from her since. Each morning Olivia sat in her bedroom chair and fixed her eyes out the window toward the east. Her heart cried out to God, *Please have the sun rise and give me hope for today.* God never failed. Each morning, the sun rose exactly at the predicted time. God's faithfulness was brilliantly displayed. It gave Olivia hope and assailed her fears. God *is* in control. If He could make the sun rise at precisely the predicted time each morning, He was able to watch over Carly and bring Olivia peace.

God is always faithful to keep His promises. He is always there for us. Even when our world or emotions seem out of control, God is always in control. He can be trusted. We can cry out to Him in our darkest hour. He is sovereign. He is enough when everything else fails. His love is constant. His mercies are new every morning.

God understands your fears. He wants to enter into your pain and provide for you. Open your heart and pour out your emotions. He can handle it. Allow God to demonstrate His faithfulness and mercy in your life. Trust Him when you're being buffeted by the storms of life. The next time you feel discouraged, downtrodden, or fearful, remember the sunrise. God *will* be faithful to you! That is who He is. The sun will rise by God's power. He will raise you and give you hope. Great is His faithfulness!

Has God ever demonstrated His faithfulness in your life? If so, how and when? If you are experiencing a difficult time right now, cry out to God for help. He will *be faithful to you!*

Look Like Jesus

Do nothing from selfish ambition or conceit,
but in humility count others more
significant than yourselves.

PHILIPPIANS 2:3

The self-made man or woman is highly esteemed in our society. Unfortunately, pride can be a by-product of success. Sometimes people with worldly success have difficulty looking like Jesus. Their material possessions or earthly achievements can become obstacles to following Him. Although their financial needs have been met, they are blind to their spiritual poverty. Money and power have puffed them up instead of making them humble.

Humility is the first prerequisite in order to look like Jesus. We must see our spiritual need of a Savior. Financial success has nothing to do with joy, peace, or contentment. Our world is full of miserable millionaires! Money and material possessions can quietly become idols. We can worship cars, homes, boats, vacations—created things rather than the Creator. Romans 1:24–25 is a warning: "Therefore God gave them up in the lusts of their hearts to impurity, to the dishonoring of their bodies among themselves, because they exchanged the truth about God for a lie and worshiped and served the creature rather than the Creator, who is blessed forever! Amen."

If you have been successful in this world, don't feel guilty. Thank the Lord. But be on guard so that the things of this world will not become stumbling blocks in your spiritual walk. A self-made man or woman does not truly exist. Everything that you possess has been given to you by God—including your ability to be successful by the world's standards. When you believe that truth and adopt that attitude, humility pushes pride aside. Fix your eyes on Jesus. Honor Him with your wealth. Bless others with the blessings that He has bestowed upon you. Then you will look more and more like Jesus regardless of your net worth.

Do you think it is easy or difficult to look like Jesus when someone has substantial financial resources? Regardless of the size of your bank account, you are rich in Christ! Remember, spiritual blessings far outweigh material ones.

What Is That to You?

Jesus said to him, "If it is my will that he remain until I come, what is that to you? You follow me!"

JOHN 21:22

Laura was an open book and readily asked her friends for prayer support. Stephanie, her best friend, had just been diagnosed with cancer. Laura could not understand Stephanie's choice to remain private and not tell many people. Venting to her husband one evening, Laura said, "I don't know why in the world Stephanie wouldn't want people to pray for her!" Bob just shrugged, but the Holy Spirit answered her with Jesus' words to Peter: "What is that to you?"

Turning to John 21, Laura read about Peter's conversation with Jesus. Jesus described the type of death Peter would have in order to glorify God. Pointing to John, Peter asked Jesus about John's death. Jesus immediately rebuked Peter and essentially told Peter that it was none of his business. Peter needed to concentrate on following Jesus, not worry about anyone else! The Holy Spirit used scripture to convict Laura and to show her that she had been judging Stephanie. It was none of Laura's business how Stephanie decided to walk through her cancer diagnosis. If Stephanie wanted to keep it private, that was her business, not Laura's!

Are you quick to judge others by your standards? Do you think that your way is the right way? Each person has the right to make their own decisions based on their personality, beliefs, and convictions. You are not their judge. Their affairs are none of your business. Think about it—there's enough on your own plate! Like Peter, you are to concentrate on following Jesus. Stay in your own lane. Respect others, and keep your eyes on Jesus.

Do you have a tendency to judge others? If so, about what? Describe a time when the Holy Spirit convicted you of something. Ask the Lord to reveal areas where you may have a judgmental attitude toward another. Confess and ask for forgiveness. Purpose to keep focused on Jesus and follow Him.

Guilty as Charged

*For all have sinned and fall short of the glory of God,
and are justified by his grace as a gift, through the
redemption that is in Christ Jesus.*

ROMANS 3:23–24

Peggy jumped behind the wheel to give her husband, Charlie, a break from driving. Suddenly Charlie yelled, "Turn left here!" Crossing three lanes of traffic, Peggy entered the intersection as the traffic light turned yellow. Realizing that her lane was ending, she sped up and blew past the car ahead of her to merge. That car just happened to be an unmarked police car! Blue lights in the rearview mirror are never good. The officer read Peggy the riot act because she had been driving like a madwoman! Although she could have blamed Charlie, she was the one behind the wheel. She was at fault—guilty as charged. The policeman gave Peggy a warning rather than a $300 ticket that day.

Not having to pay that fine reminded Peggy of God's grace. We are all sinners in God's sight and have fallen short of living a perfect life. The penalty of sin is death, but Jesus paid the penalty for us when He gave His life on Calvary. Although we are guilty as charged, our faith in Jesus brings us forgiveness and assures us of eternal life rather than the death penalty.

Just because you have been forgiven, you don't have the license to sin. Think about your Christian walk. Are you reckless or careless, like Peggy behind the wheel? You can blame others for your behavior, but ultimately you alone are responsible for your choices. Are you endangering yourself or others physically, emotionally, or spiritually? If Jesus pulled you over today, would He say, "Well done, My faithful servant" or "Guilty as charged"?

Have you acknowledged your sin before a holy God and found forgiveness in Christ? If not, accept His free gift of eternal life by faith today. How would you characterize your Christian walk? Do you take God's grace for granted, or do you live in a way that honors Him?

Older Women

Older women likewise are to be reverent in behavior,
not slanderers or slaves to much wine. They are to
teach what is good, and so train the young women
to love their husbands and children.

TITUS 2:3–4

Heading into church, Becky said hi to the elderly lady walking just ahead of her. Marilyn responded, "Hi! I don't know who it is because I can't turn around," as she continued walking slowly forward with her cane. After she passed through the doors, Marilyn was able to turn around to greet Becky. Although age had caught up with her body, Marilyn and her husband Bill faithfully attended Bible study together. Their presence was such a testimony to Becky.

Retirement. In our society we work hard and look forward to the day when we can kick back and do whatever we please. What will that day look like? Most people in their eighties might be content to rock on their front porch. Although it's extremely difficult, Marilyn and Bill make the effort to get in their car and drive to Bible study every Monday evening. They are not finished gleaning from God's Word. They value the importance of spiritual growth. God is not done with them yet, and they know it!

If you are retired, what do you enjoy doing? Regardless of your age, God is calling you into a closer walk with Him. Our society may not value older women, but God does. Older women possess godly wisdom that can be passed on to the next generation. If you are retired, be an example to those following in your footsteps. Recognize your worth in God's eyes. Inspire the younger generation as they see you still yearning to learn God's truth and to grow spiritually. As you follow Jesus, may others follow you!

What is your view on aging and retirement?
What do you envision doing as you grow older?
Is studying God's Word a priority? Has anyone served
as a godly example and role model in your life?
What are you doing to inspire the next generation?

Prepare Now

It is appointed for man to die once,
and after that comes judgment.

HEBREWS 9:27

Trekking in Nepal requires advance preparation. Proper clothing and physical conditioning are imperative! Trekkers would never think of showing up at the Yak and Yeti Hotel in Kathmandu without warm boots, jackets, gloves, and hats. Hiking in the Himalayans ill-prepared can prove to be fatal. The Christian life is no different.

Christians are on a trek—a trek through this life as we journey to our heavenly home. Are we preparing now for our eternal future? Many books and articles have been written to prepare Himalayan trekkers, but only one book, the Bible, can adequately prepare us for the future. Matthew 6:19–21 exhorts us to store up for ourselves treasures in heaven as opposed to amassing earthly treasures. In this life, it's easy to become distracted by the things of this world. We are to keep our eyes fixed on Jesus as we prepare for eternity with Him (see Hebrews 12:2). This life is not always easy. Jesus warns us that we will have trouble. Yet He also assures us that we can take heart knowing that He has overcome the world (see John 16:33).

Knowing and living by biblical truth is crucial if you are to be adequately prepared for death. Christians need not fear physical death and judgment. You have been given spiritual life through Christ. When God looks at you, He sees Christ's righteousness and declares you not guilty. You are forgiven and will be ushered into heaven. Prepare now for that glorious day! Accept Jesus as your personal Lord and Savior if you have not already done so. If you know Him now, then open your Bible daily and learn from His Word so that you can be prepared for your future spent with Him.

Are you ready to meet the Lord face-to-face? If not, why not? Talk to the Lord about this. What steps might you take to be better prepared? Are there any Bible verses that help you live today in preparation for tomorrow?

You Never Know

But if anyone has the world's goods and sees his
brother in need, yet closes his heart against him,
how does God's love abide in him? Little children,
let us not love in word or talk but
in deed and in truth.

1 JOHN 3:17–18

In her younger years, Janice tackled household projects herself. But at eighty years old, she decided to hire Jake, a handyman. Jake was a former Army Ranger who had recently divorced after twenty-five years of marriage. One afternoon as Jake was leaving, Janice asked if he could pick up something for her at Home Depot. She was shocked when he responded, "Sure, that's no problem. I sleep in my truck in the Home Depot parking lot."

We brush shoulders with people every day—the waitress at our local diner, the cashier at the checkout counter, the coworker in the next office. Do we ever stop and think about the burdens they may carry? Smiling faces can disguise hearts filled with heartache and pain. Suffering in silence, they may feel as if no one cares. Perhaps they do not know the One who loves them the most—Jesus!

Love is an action word. True love evokes a response. James 2:15–17 says, "If a brother or sister is poorly clothed and lacking in daily food, and one of you says to them, 'Go in peace, be warmed and filled,' without giving them the things needed for the body, what good is that? So also faith by itself, if it does not have works, is dead." Self-absorption closes your heart to others. Ask the Lord to open your eyes to see the needs of others. Engage them in conversation. Listen. Then be ready to respond as the Lord leads. Give financially. Pray for them. Share Jesus. Love them in truth and deed!

Do you tend to be aware or oblivious to the needs of those around you? Can you think of someone in need who could use your help? Ask God to show you how to demonstrate His love to them.

Worthless Knowledge

But be doers of the word, and not hearers only,
deceiving yourselves. For if anyone is a hearer of
the word and not a doer, he is like a man who
looks intently at his natural face in a mirror.
For he looks at himself and goes away and
at once forgets what he was like.

JAMES 1:22–24

Lynn knew that smoking could cause cancer, yet she continued to light up. Bryan acknowledged that he was fifty pounds overweight, but he enjoyed Dunkin' Donuts every morning. Jill admitted that she lived with an abusive man, yet she refused to leave or seek help. Head knowledge is worthless unless it's applied. Knowledge moves from our head to our heart when we act upon it. Then we truly own it. Only heart knowledge can bring about physical or spiritual change.

We know that we should forgive others, treat others above ourselves, not be anxious or worry, trust in the Lord and not rely on our own understanding, come to Jesus when weary and burdened, and seek first the kingdom of

God. But unless we apply it in our lives, this knowledge will fail to transform us. It will remain worthless.

Applying God's truth to your daily life is an act of the will. Obedience is choosing to follow Jesus above yourself. It's not an easy road—it requires sacrifice. You must feed on spiritual food. Open your Bible more often than *People* magazine. Enroll in a Bible study. Turn off the TV to pray more. Ask the Lord to give you the desire and ability to apply His truth. Listen to the Holy Spirit. Follow His promptings. Apply what you glean. Allow head knowledge to move to your heart. Don't allow your spiritual knowledge to become worthless. Apply it today!

Can you think of any examples of "worthless knowledge"? Are there any spiritual truths that are difficult for you to apply? Talk to the Lord about it, and ask for His help.

Declaring Truth

But as for me, I will look to the LORD; I will wait
for the God of my salvation; my God will hear me.
Rejoice not over me, O my enemy; when I fall,
I shall rise; when I sit in darkness,
the LORD will be a light to me.

MICAH 7:7–8

Fear can cripple our emotions. Struggles in life can leave us
feeling hopeless and forsaken by God. When God seems
distant, we can erroneously conclude that He doesn't care
or love us. That is simply not true. Emotions are not facts,
and they can fool us.

Many biblical examples give us hope. Joseph was sold
into slavery. King David fled for his life and hid in the
caves of En Gedi. Paul was shipwrecked. How did each of
these men feel? Had God forgotten or abandoned them?
Absolutely not! God is sovereign. He knew exactly where
they were and what was happening. God's will was fulfilled
in each of these cases in His perfect timing.

In tough times, declare God's truth in order to bring
your emotions in check. Look to the Lord and wait for

Him. God hears you. When you fall, He will lift you up. When darkness surrounds you, allow Jesus to be your light. In the Garden of Gethsemane, as Jesus was overcome with emotion, He submitted to His Father's will. Jesus died on the cross but overcame death through His resurrection. "In all these things we are more than conquerors through him who loved us. For I am sure that neither death nor life, nor angels nor rulers, nor things present nor things to come, nor powers, nor height nor depth, nor anything else in all creation, will be able to separate us from the love of God in Christ Jesus our Lord" (Romans 8:37–39). What a promise! Declare that truth in your life today!

Have you ever felt overwhelmed or hopeless? How did you respond? In hindsight, how could you have handled things differently? Do you currently need victory in your life? Go to the Lord in prayer.

Is Jesus Enough?

"Glory to God in the highest, and on earth peace among those with whom he is pleased!"

LUKE 2:14

Peggy was dreading Christmas. She and her husband would be alone for the first time—no kids, no grandkids, no huge meal to prepare. Peggy's emotions were swirling. "This just isn't going to be Christmas," she mused. The still, small voice of the Holy Spirit whispered, *"Am I enough?"* That question pierced her heart. Had she allowed her family to become an idol? Was God permitting these circumstances so that Peggy could worship Him alone?

The true celebration of Christmas is the gift of Jesus. We want to share that joy with family and friends. But it's easy to become so distracted with all the preparations that we miss Jesus. When anything usurps our enjoyment of Christ Himself, something has gone askew. God's gentle rebuke served to turn Peggy's attitude around. When everything else was taken away, Jesus remained. Peggy discovered that He was more than enough!

On that first Christmas morn, angels gave glory to

God in the highest! All the focus was on Jesus, the Christ Child, the Messiah, the Savior of the world! Jesus' coming fulfilled Isaiah's prophecy, "The Spirit of the Lord GOD is upon me, because the LORD has anointed me to bring good news to the poor; he has sent me to bind up the brokenhearted, to proclaim liberty to the captives, and the opening of the prison to those who are bound; to proclaim the year of the LORD's favor, and the day of vengeance of our God; to comfort all who mourn; to grant to those who mourn in Zion—to give them a beautiful headdress instead of ashes, the oil of gladness instead of mourning, the garment of praise instead of a faint spirit" (Isaiah 61:1–3). Jesus is more than enough! Worship Him alone. Glory to God in the highest!

What Christmas traditions do you cling to? How would you feel if things changed? How could you make Jesus the focal point, not only at Christmas but throughout the year?

You Are Ugly—
You Are Beautiful

*For you formed my inward parts; you knitted me
together in my mother's womb. I praise you,
for I am fearfully and wonderfully made.*

Psalm 139:13–14

The world constantly shouts, "You are ugly!" Look at the airbrushed models in magazines or the cosmetically enhanced movie stars. Even women over sixty appear wrinkle-free! Yet when we look in the mirror, the furrow lines between our brows jump out at us. Our arms are too flabby and our neck resembles a chicken's! Ugly! In today's world it's easy to obsess over reversing the aging process. We spend so much time and money on cosmetics, creams, injections, exercise—anything to erase the word *ugly* that stares back at us in the mirror.

Yet Creator God continues to whisper, "*You are beautiful!*" The Lord God Almighty made us, and we are beautiful in His sight. He looks past our wrinkles and aging body to our heart and soul. That is His focus and how He assesses our beauty. As the prophet Samuel was selecting the next king of Israel, the Lord reminded him, "For the LORD sees not as man sees; man looks on the outward appearance, but the LORD looks on the heart" (1 Samuel 16:7).

Your focus should be a transformed heart rather than a transformed face. Proverbs 31:30 says, "Charm is deceitful, and beauty is vain, but a woman who fears the LORD is to be praised." Staying fit and healthy is wise. However, aging is inevitable. Spend your time cultivating inward beauty rather than chasing after elusive outward beauty. The more you do that, the louder God's voice will become. Which voice will you listen to—the world's that says you are ugly or God's that affirms your beauty? Believe the Lord—you are beautiful in His sight, and that's all that really matters!

Do you struggle with feeling beautiful? What are some ways that you can focus on inward rather than outward beauty? If you have a poor body image, ask God to give you faith to see yourself as He does.

Pretty-Ugly

But God shows his love for us in that while we were still sinners, Christ died for us.

ROMANS 5:8

Read the following from top to bottom. Then start at the bottom and read up.

I'm very ugly
So don't try to convince me that
I am a very beautiful person
Because at the end of the day
I hate myself in every single way
And I'm not going to lie to myself by saying
There is beauty inside of me that matters
So rest assured I will remind myself
That I am a worthless, unlovable person
And nothing you say will make me believe
I am loved
Because no matter what
I am not good enough to be loved
And I am in no position to believe that

Beauty exists within me
Because whenever I look in the mirror I always think
Am I as ugly as people say?
(Author Unknown)

You may feel ugly. You may act ugly. But in God's sight you are beautiful! You are loved unconditionally by your heavenly Father. Let that sink in. God loved you *so much* that He sent His Son, Jesus, to die for you. So don't call yourself ugly if Jesus deemed you worthy to die for! That is how much you are loved! Jesus poured out His grace on the cross—giving you what you don't deserve because of His love for you. You deserved death because of your ugly sin. Yet Jesus took your punishment as He hung on the cross. You don't deserve it, yet you can receive it by faith. You are loved by God. What more affirmation do you need? Receive His love by faith. Be forgiven. Shine as a beautiful testimony of His love.

Whenever you start feeling low and down on yourself,
remember how beautiful you are in God's sight!
Meditate on the truth that Jesus died for you.
What greater demonstration of love is there?

The Lord of Lords

He who is the blessed and only Sovereign, the King of kings and Lord of lords, who alone has immortality, who dwells in unapproachable light, whom no one has ever seen or can see. To him be honor and eternal dominion. Amen.

1 TIMOTHY 6:15–16

God gave parents authority over their children. "Children, obey your parents in the Lord, for this is right" (Ephesians 6:1). Yet some parents would rather be their child's best friend. Unacceptable behavior and whining are tolerated. When discipline is lacking, the child puts himself in charge.

Believers enjoy a close, intimate relationship with Jesus. Although He calls us friend, do we expect Him to tolerate unacceptable, sinful behavior? Like spoiled children, do we whine, grumble, or argue with Him? Do we pitch a fit when we don't get our own way? Have we put ourselves in charge? "Woe to him who strives with him who formed him, a pot among earthen pots! Does the clay say to him who forms it, 'What are you making?'" (Isaiah 45:9).

Jesus will not be manipulated by anyone. He doesn't cave in to suit your whims. Jesus is wiser and knows what's best for you, so He holds firm. He disciplines you for your own good. Jesus is the Lord of lords and King of kings—God Almighty! The book of Revelation portrays Jesus as our coming King, the ruler of an eternal kingdom. Jesus was there in Genesis when the world was created, and He will come again at the end of the age. As you get a glimpse of His power and might, may you fall down in worship. Honor and glory belong to Him alone. He is God, not you! May you not become so casual that you fail to acknowledge His lordship. Worship the King of kings and Lord of lords today!

Describe your relationship with Jesus. Is it close and personal, or does He seem distant? Although He is your friend, He is to be revered and worshipped. Ask the Lord to help you gain this proper perspective.

The Blind Side

The wise of heart will receive commandments,
but a babbling fool will come to ruin.

PROVERBS 10:8

Football quarterbacks have a blind side. Since most are right-handed, defenders coming from their left are more difficult to see. Taking advantage of this weakness, a quick defensive end can sack a quarterback before he knows what hit him! That's why the left tackle is such a key position. The left tackle protects his quarterback's vulnerable side.

All of us have blind sides in the game of life. We are knocked to our knees by something we never saw coming. Love may compel us to enable a loved one, yet we are blind to their manipulation. We may be attracted to men who use and abuse us because we are so desperate for love. Anger may spew out of our mouths at the end of the day when we've hit a brick wall. Why do we keep doing these things? We are blind to the signs that have led us to where we find ourselves. Like the quarterback lying on the ground, we scramble to stand back up.

Thankfully, God has given us one another. You may be

able to see clearly what a friend is unable to discern—and vice versa. Don't allow pride to prevent you from inviting someone to be your left tackle when you desperately need protection. Trust a close friend or spouse. Give them permission to speak truth to you. Allow them to point out the red flags that you cannot see. Could you be in a codependent relationship with your child? Would you benefit from spiritual counseling to determine why you feel unlovable? Do you tend to get angry when you're tired and hungry? Be wise. Be open to instruction. Draft a left tackle to minimize your blind side so that you won't fall flat on your face!

Have you ever been blindsided? Does it keep happening? Do you have a trusted friend or spouse who helps protect your weak areas? If not, consider confiding in a close friend. Be each other's "left tackle" to protect one another from being blindsided.

Foxhole Faith

"Go and cry out to the gods whom you have chosen;
let them save you in the time of your distress."

JUDGES 10:14

The Israelites rode a spiritual roller coaster: rebellion, discipline, repentance, deliverance, rebellion. In good times, they forgot God. Pride, disobedience, and stubbornness prevailed. When God disciplined them, they cried out for deliverance. In Judges 10, the Israelites served other gods. God handed them over to the Philistines and Ammonites who crushed and oppressed them. In their distress, they cried out to the Lord. The verse above reveals God's emotional response.

The Israelites only seemed to cry out to God when they were in trouble. They wanted to live life their own way until it became difficult. Then they expected God to rescue them. God longed for a mutually loving relationship where they trusted and followed Him alone. They refused. They only repented of their sin and rebellion when severe trials came their way. Did God feel used? Did He feel that the Israelites were only turning to Him

166

because they needed something from Him?

What about you? Do you walk closely with the Lord in good times and bad? Or are you on a spiritual roller coaster? Like the soldier in the foxhole, do you only cry out to God when bullets are whizzing past your head? God is gracious and full of mercy. He hears your cries for help and responds. Adversity may draw you near to Him, but His heart's desire is that you remain there. Realize that you always need the Lord—in good times and bad. Learn from the Israelites. Do not become prideful and arrogant when life is going well. Walk closely with the Lord always. Do not use Him for your own purposes, but be used by the Lord for His!

Have you ever been on a spiritual roller coaster? How did the Lord get your attention when you strayed? Do you have a friend or family member who only calls when they need your help? Now apply that to your relationship with God. Write down your thoughts.

Simple Yet Difficult

*"If you love me, you will keep
my commandments."*

JOHN 14:15

Jesus made this simple yet difficult statement. Jesus says that our love is demonstrated through obedience. Obedience is not easy because it requires an attitude of submission. We must desire to follow Him rather than our own way. Sometimes His ways are difficult to discern. Our heart must be in tune with His will.

The Bible is paramount in helping us obey Jesus. The more we read God's Word, the more it transforms our hearts. As the world pulls us one way, Jesus asks us to go in the opposite direction. Romans 12:2 encourages: "Do not be conformed to this world, but be transformed by the renewal of your mind, that by testing you may discern what is the will of God, what is good and acceptable and perfect." Our minds are renewed as we read and meditate on scripture. God's truth exposes lies, and we begin to gain God's perspective. Learning to listen to the promptings of the Holy Spirit—the still, quiet voice—is essential to following Him.

Jesus commands you to forgive others. If you love Jesus, you will extend forgiveness to a friend who has betrayed you. Make the difficult phone call to reach out and bring reconciliation. Jesus commands you not to judge others. The next time you see yourself as superior to another, confess your thoughts and extend a smile or kind word instead. Obedience is difficult, but the good news is that God wants to help you walk in His ways. We find encouragement in Philippians 2:13: "For it is God who works in you, both to will and to work for his good pleasure." Demonstrate your love of Jesus by keeping His commandments! He will help you do it!

How do you demonstrate your love of Jesus? What do you find more difficult—having a submissive attitude or discerning His will in order to follow in obedience? Have you been disobedient in an area of your life? Confess it now, and ask God to help you follow Him.

God's World or Our World

*The earth is the LORD's and the fullness thereof,
the world and those who dwell therein,
for he has founded it upon the seas
and established it upon the rivers.*

PSALM 24:1–2

In 1901 Maltbie Babcock proclaimed that God is not only Creator but also sustainer and ruler of the world when he penned the lyrics to the song "This Is My Father's World." What do you believe? If it's God's world, then He is in control and we aim to serve Him. If we believe it's our world, then we are in control and God is here to serve us.

The truth is this is God's world. For proof, read Genesis 1:1: "In the beginning, God created the heavens and the earth." Out of nothing, God made everything! He not only made the sun, moon, stars, plants, and animals—He made us! Therefore, He is the One in charge and in control. This is His world and rightly so. He made it; we didn't. Why are we so quick to forget that important fact?

Satan was originally an angel created by God. But Satan wasn't content with just being an angel. He wanted to be worshipped as God. When he tried to usurp God's authority, he was cast out of heaven as a fallen angel (see Isaiah 14:12–15 and Ezekiel 28:12–19). Satan even tempted Jesus to bow down and worship him (see Matthew 4:8–10). Satan still tries to usurp God's authority by convincing you that this is *your* world, not God's. Satan lies and says that you should be in control. Don't be fooled. Don't try to usurp Creator God's rightful place. He is Creator. He is sovereign. This *is* His world!

Do you think this is God's world or yours?
Think about your last few days. Were you trying to
control things and expecting God to bless your plans?
Then perhaps you have erroneously concluded that
it's your world and you're the one in charge.
Put God back on the throne of your life.
Worship Creator God and thank
Him for His world!

For God So Loved

"For God so loved the world, that he gave his only Son, that whoever believes in him should not perish but have eternal life."

JOHN 3:16

Although Bonnie was familiar with John 3:16, she still felt unlovable. Poor life choices had left her feeling worthless and ashamed. Cultivating relationships was difficult—until she met Bryan. Bonnie and Bryan had a lot in common, with the exception that Bryan's parents were professing Christians. They emulated God's unconditional love toward Bonnie. God used Bryan's parents to help Bonnie believe that she could be loved. After many years, Bonnie received God's love into her heart and believed that Jesus died for even her!

Yes, God loves the world—that means every single person in it. There is *no one* beyond His love. There is *no one* who has fallen or strayed too far. There is *no one* God's love excludes. The Bible is full of testimonies of God's redeeming power and grace in the lives of imperfect people. God loves those who feel unlovable.

You may *feel* unlovable, but you *are* loved! God's truth declares that God loves you so much that He sent Jesus to die on the cross and give His life for you! There is no greater love than that. Jesus says in John 10:10, "I came that they may have life and have it abundantly." Jesus came not only to give you eternal life with Him in heaven, but to give you an abundant life on earth with Him today. Embrace His love, and walk with Him throughout the day. Thank Him for His indescribable gift! Is there someone you might share His love with today?

Do you know how much you are loved by God? Have you accepted His unconditional love for you? Do you feel undeserving? We all are! Broken? That's exactly who God loves. Don't allow any sin to stand in the way of accepting Jesus as your Savior. He came to die for your sin and offer you forgiveness. Embrace His love today!

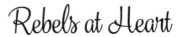

Rebels at Heart

Submit yourselves therefore to God.
Resist the devil, and he will flee from you.

JAMES 4:7

No is a small yet powerful word. By two years of age, most children have this word mastered. Children verbally rebel against anyone standing in the way of their desires as they strive for autonomy. As children mature, they are taught that there *are* appropriate times to say no. For example, when a stranger offers them a ride or when someone tempts them to use drugs.

Rebellion is resistance, defiance, or disobedience. It comes naturally to all of us. We were born rebels, yearning to go our own way. Our rebellion against God is described in Isaiah 53:6: "All we like sheep have gone astray; we have turned—every one—to his own way; and the LORD has laid on him the iniquity of us all." Even though we are rebels, God loves us and sent His Son to redeem us. What amazing love! This should compel us to follow Him wherever He might lead us.

Unfortunately, you have an adversary, Satan, who

lies in order to convince you that God is standing in the way of your happiness. Satan tempts you to rebel against God in order to follow him. But what if you decided to rebel against Satan instead? What if you turned the tables and resisted the devil in order to go God's way? Satan may lie and tempt you, but if you stand firm on God's truth, Satan must flee. The choice is yours. You can rebel against God in order to go your own way, or you can rebel against Satan in order to go God's way. It's a life-or-death decision. Choose life. Rebel against Satan. Resist him and stand firm on God's Word. Trust in the power of the Holy Spirit to sustain you.

Have you ever considered yourself a rebel? In what ways have you rebelled against God? What were the results? Have you ever resisted Satan? Describe the circumstances; what were the results? Experience victory by saying no to Satan.

Milk vs. Meat

For though by this time you ought to be teachers, you need someone to teach you again the basic principles of the oracles of God. You need milk, not solid food, for everyone who lives on milk is unskilled in the word of righteousness, since he is a child. But solid food is for the mature, for those who have their powers of discernment trained by constant practice to distinguish good from evil.

Hebrews 5:12–14

Our physical bodies go through a maturation process from infancy to adulthood. Babies are incapable of eating or digesting steak. And teenagers should have progressed past drinking milk from a baby bottle!

Our spiritual bodies go through a similar progression. When we first become Christians, we are spiritual babies. We need to feed on elementary spiritual truths found in God's Word. "Like newborn infants, long for the pure spiritual milk, that by it you may grow up into salvation" (1 Peter 2:2). First we learn basic truths: we are saved by grace, not by works; God has forgiven our past, present, and future sins; nothing can separate us from God's love. When we apply what we learn, we mature spiritually.

Solid spiritual food is for the mature Christian who can discern deeper doctrine because of having been trained by constant practice. Maturity is a process that doesn't happen overnight. Don't get stuck in the infant stage forever. If you have been a Christian for years, don't be content to drink from a spiritual bottle or be spoon-fed. Open the Bible for yourself on a daily basis. Go deeper. Challenge yourself further. Apply hard truths in your daily life. As you mature and graduate from spiritual milk to spiritual meat, you will be able to feast at God's spiritual banquet table!

Would you describe yourself as a spiritual babe or mature believer? What are some ways that you have applied God's truth and seen spiritual growth as a result? Are you satisfied with your spiritual maturity? If not, how might you grow? Is your current church challenging you spiritually? If not, consider finding one that does.

Open My Eyes, Lord

"For I was hungry and you gave me food, I was thirsty and you gave me drink, I was a stranger and you welcomed me. . . . As you did it to one of the least of these my brothers, you did it to me."

On her way to the grocery store, Marlene passed a man holding up a cardboard sign. *Is he really homeless? If I gave him money for food, would he buy drugs instead?* Cringing at her thoughts, Marlene asked God to open her eyes to whom she should help. Beautiful music wafted through the air as she stepped out of her car in the parking lot. A young man played a saxophone next to the store entrance. The Lord tugged on her heart as if to say, *"Him!"* The musician glowed ear to ear as Marlene dropped some money into his open saxophone case lying at his feet. After shopping, Marlene walked with the bagger to her car. She learned that he was from Iran. Again God seemed to whisper, *"Him!"* When she tipped him as he unloaded her groceries, he spontaneously gave her a huge bear hug! It was as if she had just handed him a million dollars!

Helping can actually hurt if it enables someone to continue destructive behavior or prevents them from assuming personal responsibility. But many people truly need food, shelter, and more importantly God's love. Ask the Lord to open your eyes. Ask Him for wisdom and discernment. Then when you hear His still, small voice—act! Realize that whatever you do for others, you are doing for the Lord. We serve Christ by serving others. May He open your eyes while you hold out the Bread of Life and the Living Water to a hungry and thirsty world!

How have you helped those in need? How do you discern whom God is calling you to help? This week ask God to open your eyes to someone who needs your help. Then act on His promptings. What happened?

When One Plus One Equals Three

Trust in the LORD with all your heart, and do not lean on your own understanding. In all your ways acknowledge him, and he will make straight your paths.

PROVERBS 3:5–6

Marsha had her whole life planned out. She would marry Brett after college, have two children, and live happily ever after. Marsha and Brett did marry and have two children, but the happily ever after came to a screeching halt when her children became teenagers. She assumed that if her children were raised in a loving, Christian home they would follow God's ways. So Marsha was shocked when her son turned to drugs and her daughter became pregnant out of wedlock. This was not supposed to happen!

Life rarely turns out the way we envisioned. We erroneously believe that we can control outcomes in life. When anger or disillusionment surfaces, our true attitudes are exposed. But who are we? When one plus one equals three, we face the stark reality that we are not sovereign. We are not in control. We are not God.

God is at work even when things don't turn out according to your plan. God is at work even in your pain. He asks you to trust Him. You cannot control anyone's choices but your own. God is asking you to completely surrender to His plan and what He is doing. Cling to this lifeline: "And we know that for those who love God all things work together for good, for those who are called according to his purpose" (Romans 8:28). God is faithful and does not lie. He will work *all things* together for good when you walk in His purpose. Pray for your loved ones, and release them to God. He will make your paths straight when you do.

Has life ever thrown you a curveball that you never expected? How did you react? Do you tend to try to control life, or do you allow God control? How might you trust God with a current situation and not lean on your own understanding? Pray about that now.

Nothing Is Wasted

To grant to those who mourn in Zion—to give them a beautiful headdress instead of ashes, the oil of gladness instead of mourning, the garment of praise instead of a faint spirit; that they may be called oaks of righteousness, the planting of the LORD, that he may be glorified.

ISAIAH 61:3

Keri moved in with Jason in hopes that marriage would soon follow. The "soon" never happened. Four years later Keri moved out feeling used, betrayed, and stupid. In desperation she returned to church in search of answers. As she began reading her Bible again, Keri was met by Jesus. He wrapped His loving arms around her, comforted her, and wiped her tears. He did not condemn her for going her own way. Instead, He welcomed her back.

Our choices in life may take us down a road that leads us away from the Lord into a dark place. We may feel lost, but God knows exactly where we are! We are never lost to Him. Sometimes He allows us to go our own way so that we discover a dead-end road apart from Him. Those dead ends ignite a yearning in our souls, and we cry out to be saved and rescued. As we turn to the Lord, He is always standing there with open arms.

Nothing in your life is ever wasted. Even your mistakes and rebellion can be used to bring you back to God. He can bring beauty from the ash heaps of your life. God wants to replace mourning with joy and despair with praise. Turn to Him when you feel disillusioned and confused. Allow Him to wipe your tears and comfort your heart. God loves you unconditionally and wants to bind your wounds. He is the only One who can bring something good from the messes you make. Invite Him in. Receive His joy and peace. Remember—nothing is wasted!

When you have made a mess of things, do you typically run away from the Lord or toward Him? Why? Has God ever turned the ashes in your life into something beautiful?

God's Side

Every way of a man is right in his own eyes,
but the LORD weighs the heart.

PROVERBS 21:2

Russell and Brenda were both ready to throw in the marriage towel. Brenda accused Russell of withdrawing into his own little world, while Russell thought Brenda was trying to control his every move. Both felt unloved and unappreciated. They each believed that their marital problems were the other person's fault.

Everyone feels justified in their own mind. However, there are two sides to everything. And then there is God's side, the side of absolute truth. We are all flawed and prideful. We perceive life from our point of view, but God sees things as they truly are. Isaiah 55:8–9 says: "For my thoughts are not your thoughts, neither are your ways my ways, declares the LORD. For as the heavens are higher than the earth, so are my ways higher than your ways and my thoughts than your thoughts." He knows our hearts. He knows our thoughts and attitudes. Our outward actions may seem aligned with His ways, but if our motives or attitudes are not, we are only deceiving ourselves.

Look in the mirror of God's Word. Acknowledge reality. Quit trying to deny truth or blame others. Take personal responsibility to walk before God with integrity and obedience. Regardless of how hard you try, you cannot change someone else. But you can allow the Lord free rein to change you—to transform your heart into His likeness. Come over to God's side by walking in truth and taking responsibility for your actions, attitudes, and motives. Be honest with yourself, and quit being deceived. You can't live the Christian life with integrity apart from the control of the indwelling Holy Spirit. But first you must relinquish control through humility. Desire to be on God's side rather than holding on with pride to your own perspective.

In personal relationships, is it difficult for you to believe that you could be wrong? Is conflict always someone else's fault? If so, read and meditate on Psalm 139:23–24.

Bossiness

What causes quarrels and what causes fights among you? Is it not this, that your passions are at war within you? You desire and do not have, so you murder. You covet and cannot obtain, so you fight and quarrel. You do not have, because you do not ask. You ask and do not receive, because you ask wrongly, to spend it on your passions.

JAMES 4:1–3

Becca's mother was exasperated with her five-year-old. Whenever Becca's friends came over to play, Becca insisted on bossing them around. If they refused to comply, Becca would become angry and argumentative. Fast-forward thirty years—Becca still had to be in control. Her marriage was in shambles because of her bossiness.

It's human nature to demand our own way. Pride prevents us from seeing another's perspective and blinds us to our own attitudes. Most of us assume that we are right and others are wrong. Bossy people overtly demonstrate that attitude. However, covert tactics such as sulking, manipulating, or heaping guilt on others are equally controlling. This is not how God wants us to behave because we're acting as if we are God. There is only one God, and He is not us!

God wants you to submit to His leadership and authority. He is the boss. When you allow Him to be in control, you don't have to be. Allow others to be accountable to God, not to you. You are not their judge. Only God knows what's best. As you surrender to His will, He will provide what you need. James 4:10 says, "Humble yourselves before the Lord, and he will exalt you." The antidote to bossiness is humility. Bossiness repels others. Humility draws them. Ask God to examine your heart. Are you trying to control others? If so, submit to God and allow Him to control you. He is worthy to be the leader!

Do you ever attempt to control others? Do you use overt or covert tactics? Is there one relationship that you wish were better? Pray for God's wisdom for a more harmonious relationship.

Peace

For he himself is our peace.

EPHESIANS 2:14

The atmosphere was tense as the crash cart was pulled adjacent to the Isolette. Megan, a twenty-five-week-old preemie, had pulled out her ET tube and her oxygen saturation level was dropping rapidly. Megan's grandmother, Ann, chose to remain by her side. Although Ann knew the seriousness of the situation, she calmly rested in Jesus' presence. Miraculously the nurses were able to reinsert the tube. Knowing that the outcome could have easily been different, they rushed to hug Ann. One nurse asked her, "How could you remain so calm?" All Ann could utter was, "The Lord."

Megan's story is true. God's peace can be experienced in the most terrifying and emotional situations. If Ann would have let her mind race to what might happen, she would have run out of the room in tears. Instead, Ann trusted the Lord. Regardless of the outcome, she knew that He would never leave or forsake them.

Whatever battles or trials you face, you never face

them alone. Jesus is in the NICUs of life with you. Jesus was with Shadrach, Meshach, and Abednego in the fiery furnace, and He remains with you (see Daniel 3). That does not mean that the outcomes in life are always good. It means that regardless of the outcomes, Jesus can impart peace. You can rest knowing that He is in control. You can take comfort in knowing that even if the worst happens, He will be there to wipe your tears and give you strength. When you trust Jesus, He imparts peace. Remember that the next time you find yourself in a scary situation. He Himself is our peace! There is nothing in this life that can take Him from you. And He is truly all that you need.

What is peace? Describe a time when you experienced God's peace in the midst of a scary situation. Do you think peace is possible even if the outcome is not what you had hoped? Is it possible to have peace amid tears, pain, and grief? Explain your thoughts.

Self-Awareness

Faithful are the wounds of a friend;
profuse are the kisses of an enemy.

PROVERBS 27:6

Unfortunately, self-awareness is a skill that many have yet to develop. They inaccurately judge their own behavior and are oblivious to how it affects others. Friends and family may be hesitant to confront them for fear of reprisal. So they live in their own fantasy world while everyone around them walks on eggshells and keeps their mouth shut.

Could that describe us? How is our self-awareness? Are we oblivious to how we come across to others? A true friend may be able to see what we cannot. Friends can tell us hard truth. They are honest when assessing our behavior and attitude. When we've gone too far, they speak up. In a healthy marriage, spouses keep each other in check. No one is an island. We need one another.

Do you have a close friend with whom you feel comfortable asking for honest feedback? Consider that they may be able to see what you cannot. What areas of your behavior or attitude should you ask God to help with?

How do you come across to others? Are friends afraid to speak up for fear that you'll immediately become defensive or hostile? The wounds of a friend may hurt initially, but God can use friends to speak truth to your heart. Weigh their words against scripture to discern if there is merit in what they share. Ask God to change your heart so that it will look more like His. Be open with honest friends, and thank God for them. We grow spiritually and relationally when we align ourselves with truth. And friends can help us become more self-aware.

Do you have a close friend who can tell you the truth about yourself? Can you do the same for them? Has this strengthened or put a wedge in your relationship? Self-awareness is good; however, God's assessment of us is the best. Ask God to assess your behaviors and attitudes to see if change is needed. Then give Him permission to transform you from the inside out.

No Words

Jesus wept.
JOHN 11:35

Lazarus was ill. Desperate for help, his sisters Mary and Martha sent word to their close friend Jesus. Instead of dropping what He was doing to hurry to Bethany, Jesus decided to stay two more days. By the time Jesus came, not only had Lazarus died, but he had been in the tomb for four days! Although Jesus knew that He was planning to raise Lazarus back to life and demonstrate His deity, no one else understood that. Mary was weeping—the crowd of Jews were weeping. Jesus was "deeply moved in his spirit and greatly troubled" (John 11:33). All Jesus could do was weep with them. No words were adequate.

Life can be extremely difficult. Tragedy and heartache can rush in unannounced and leave us reeling. Death can claim the life of an unborn infant or an elderly mother. Broken marriages, rebellious children, or financial ruin can be devastating. Even if we are walking closely with the Lord, He may initially feel distant when our heart is shattered. Like Mary and Martha, we find our raw emotions screaming that if Jesus were here, this would not have happened! Take heart. He is here. He does care. He does love you. Sometimes His ways are beyond our understanding. Sometimes there are no words that can take away the pain—only tears.

When friends or loved ones encounter tragedies, you may want to help but have no idea what to say. Don't worry. Realize that there is nothing you can say to take away their pain. But don't stay away. Reach out. Let them know you care. Compassion can be demonstrated in many ways. Leave a message that you are praying for them. Sit with them and listen. Weep with them if appropriate. When there are no words, just be there. Your presence speaks volumes.

Have you ever experienced a devastating loss or tragedy? How did you react? When others are struggling, do not let your lack of words keep you from demonstrating empathy. Ask God how you might reach out to show that you care.

There Is Hope

Why are you cast down, O my soul, and why are you in turmoil within me? Hope in God; for I shall again praise him, my salvation and my God.

PSALM 42:5–6

Linda and her husband, Jim, had been married for thirty years. Jim was a successful financial advisor and Linda had devoted herself to homeschooling their children. Life appeared to be perfect—until it wasn't. Within a matter of months, the financial markets took a nosedive, cutting their personal income in half. Stress and anxiety permeated their home. Their oldest son flunked out of college. Then Linda's mother passed away unexpectedly. Linda and Jim felt hopeless and lost. What had happened to the life they once knew? Would their future ever be bright again?

We can place our hope in many things: financial security, health, family. But when we trust in these earthly treasures, our hope becomes transient and illusive. Hope in temporal things can fluctuate as those anchors shift. The financial markets go up and down. Our health can suddenly fail. Family dynamics can change. When our hope is in Jesus, we have a sure foundation. Nothing can permanently shake us because Jesus is the anchor that never moves. "Jesus Christ is the same yesterday and today and forever" (Hebrews 13:8).

There is hope—and His name is Jesus! He doesn't guarantee financial prosperity or optimal health. Having Jesus doesn't mean that your children will never struggle. But it does mean that your hope in Jesus will withstand any trial, hardship, or tragedy. Because Jesus is with you in the storms of life, you will come through. Your future is secure with Him. Isn't that what hope is? A better to-morrow? Victory? Good triumphing over evil? Put your hope in the Lord Jesus. He will prove Himself faithful, and you will praise Him yet again!

What is your hope based on? Has your world ever been shaken? What happened, and how did you handle it? Place your hope in Jesus today so that you will be prepared for adversity tomorrow.

Riches Can Make It Harder

And Jesus looked around and said to his disciples,
"How difficult it will be for those who have
wealth to enter the kingdom of God!"

MARK 10:23

Jesus' parable of the rich fool is recorded in Luke 12. When the rich man's land produced an abundance of crops, he decided to tear down his old barns and build larger ones to store his grain. Then he would relax, eat, drink, and be merry. Jesus rebuked him by calling him a fool. That very night he would die, leaving his material wealth behind. Where would his soul spend eternity?

Riches are deceptive. Possessing material wealth may lead us to believe that we lack for nothing because we are financially independent. But someday we will die and all that we have accumulated will stay here—not a penny will enter heaven. Money can blind us so that we're unable to see our need of Jesus. People in third-world countries are quite aware of their material poverty. Their attitude of neediness serves as an open door for the Gospel message. Riches have not become their god.

Money is not an idol they worship.

Why would you choose to gain the whole world, yet forfeit your very soul? Regardless of your economic or social standing, choosing Jesus is far greater. He alone gives eternal life. When your earthly treasures are someday left behind, you will be ushered into the kingdom of God! Those valued possessions will pale in comparison with the heavenly treasures that await you! Don't allow riches to get in the way of pursuing Jesus. He alone is the lover of your soul! May you love Jesus more than riches. If you have been blessed financially, use these material gifts to further His eternal kingdom!

Do you think riches can make it harder to enter the kingdom of God? Explain. Have you ever struggled with having too much or having too little? How did it affect your relationship with God? Have finances become a stumbling block in your spiritual walk? Talk to God about this.

Generosity

As for the rich in this present age, charge them not to be haughty, nor to set their hopes on the uncertainty of riches, but on God, who richly provides us with everything to enjoy. They are to do good, to be rich in good works, to be generous and ready to share, thus storing up treasure for themselves as a good foundation for the future, so that they may take hold of that which is truly life.

1 Timothy 6:17–19

God lavishes His love upon us, richly providing for our needs. He calls us to follow in His footsteps—to be generous toward others, giving of our time, talents, and resources. All that we have comes from God. Our very life and each breath we take are gifts from Him. God is pleased when we desire to pass on to others the blessings that He has bestowed upon us.

But there is a rub. By nature we are selfish, and generosity requires putting others' needs above our own. Sacrifice is required. Many times we are so absorbed in our own agenda that there is little time left over for others.

We hoard financial resources and are unwilling to let go. Or we may find ourselves in financial debt because we've purchased things that we think we can't live without. Generosity toward others seems like an illusion when we can barely keep our own head above water financially.

Generosity is an attitude of the heart. It demonstrates your belief that God is in control and will provide for you. This enables you to pass on what God has generously given you. Manage your time, talents, and financial resources well. Be a good steward of what God has entrusted to you. Be willing to sacrifice for others as an act of worship. Generosity results in heavenly treasures—eternal rewards. Then you will take hold of life that is "truly life"!

Are you by nature a generous person? Do you tend to be more generous with your time, talents, or financial resources? What steps might you take to become more generous?

God's Side

*If any of you lacks wisdom, let him ask God,
who gives generously to all without
reproach, and it will be given him.*

JAMES 1:5

There are two sides to everything. . .and then there's God's side. We typically look at life from our own perspective and assume that we are correct. But other people have different thoughts and opinions. And guess what—they believe that they are right too! Which way is it? Relational conflicts arise when we hold tightly to our side and dismiss another's point of view. How do we resolve conflicts and come together with mutual respect?

James 1:5 encourages us to ask God for wisdom. But that won't happen unless we first admit that we lack wisdom. In humility we must admit our need and acknowledge that "I could be wrong and may not know everything." Pride insists, "I am right," and "I have all the answers." Logically we could deduce that we cannot be right 100 percent of the time. Yet pride often blinds us to that truth. We must confess our pride before we're capable of receiving truth.

God is the only One with true wisdom. You may be smart, but God Almighty is omniscient. His side is the one that counts. Purpose to see life from God's perspective, because truth is on His side. Christians are not exempt from having conflicts with one another. But there is a solution when opinions differ. Both parties can ask for God's wisdom in the situation. It is a beautiful reality when two hearts align with His wisdom instead of insisting upon their own way. The next time you lack wisdom, admit it. Then ask God for His wisdom, and it will be given to you. It's a promise!

Do you admit when you're wrong, or do you tend to argue your case? Have you ever asked God for wisdom? How did God answer your prayer? Are you presently experiencing any relational conflicts? Allow the Lord to examine your heart to determine if pride is the culprit. Then in humility seek the Lord's solution.

Being Mad at God

How long, O LORD? Will you forget me forever?
How long will you hide your face from me?
How long must I take counsel in my soul
and have sorrow in my heart all the day?

PSALM 13:1–2

The unexpected phone call rocked Lucy's world forever. Her godly mother had been diagnosed with inoperative lung cancer. Lucy immediately felt anger toward God for allowing this to happen. As reality began to sink in, she realized that her mother's journey would be difficult. They could either walk it alone or with the Lord's help. Lucy admitted that she needed God now like never before. With tears flowing down her cheeks, she threw herself at His feet and confessed her anger. To her amazement, God received her lovingly. Lucy's soul was overwhelmed by God's unconditional love.

Job layoff, death, divorce, and illness are life-changing events that send us reeling. When life doesn't go according to our plans, it's easy to blame God and become angry with Him. We rationalize that since He could have intervened but didn't, it's all His fault. Church attendance, Bible reading, or prayer time may wane as we struggle to understand God's ways.

The truth is that we live in an imperfect, fallen world. The ripple effects of sin touch us all. Life happens. Heartache comes. Disappointment abounds. It's not God's fault. If God is allowing trials in your life, they have a divine purpose. God wants to help you through. He wants to be there for you and give you strength. He desires to grow your faith as you experience His faithfulness in the storms of life. So run toward Him, not away from Him! You desperately need Him. And if you get angry with God, realize that He is big enough to handle your honest emotions. But then unclench your fist and cry out to God for help. He's the only One who can truly help in your greatest hour of need.

Have you ever been mad at God?
When going through trials, do you instinctively
run toward or away from God?

Out of Our Comfort Zone

You keep him in perfect peace whose mind is
stayed on you, because he trusts in you.

ISAIAH 26:3

Megan sat at the kitchen table leafing through her mail. Little did she know that her life was about to take a dramatic turn. Missionary Ventures had sent a mailer requesting surgical personnel for a medical mission trip to Guyana. Megan sensed the Lord whispering as He tapped her shoulder. *"I want you to go."* Because His call seemed so clear, she responded in obedience. However, as departure time drew closer, her initial excitement turned to fear. She would be leaving her family and familiar surroundings to go to an unknown place with people she had never met! What was she thinking?! As encouragement, her family wrote the words of Isaiah 26:3 on a huge banner and hung it in the kitchen. That promise calmed her fears. She was able to step out of her comfort zone by trusting the Lord.

It can be frightening when the Lord asks us to attempt something new or to go to an unknown place. We like functioning in our "comfort zone" where our environment is predictable. But sometimes God orchestrates a job change, a move, or a mission trip. How do we respond? Do we continue to cling to our familiar surroundings, or are we obedient to His call? Change is scary for all of us!

Trust the Lord when you are called out of your comfort zone. He will lead and provide for you. "He will not leave you or forsake you" (Deuteronomy 31:6). God will never abandon you! Keep your mind focused on Him rather than all the unknowns. Remember: what might be unknown to you is known to God! You can experience perfect peace in the great unknown when you obediently step out in faith and trust God.

Has the Lord ever called you to step out of your comfort zone? Was it easy or difficult? If the Lord is asking you to follow Him in some way now, trust Him, and experience His peace.

Learning to Listen

Make me to know your ways, O LORD; teach me
your paths. Lead me in your truth and teach
me, for you are the God of my salvation;
for you I wait all the day long.

PSALM 25:4–5

Megan was utterly amazed at how much she felt God's presence in Guyana. Although the surgical team had just met, they functioned as if they had worked together for years! The facilities and supplies were archaic, yet they learned to improvise. The Lord gave them wisdom and insight moment by moment. Upon her return, Megan yearned to hear God as clearly in familiar surroundings as she had heard Him in Guyana. She wanted to continue that close walk with God. Wondering if that was possible, Megan began her journey in learning to listen to God.

When God takes us to unknown places, we may feel lost, disoriented, and frightened. Looking for stability and direction, we can turn to many things—some good, others not so good. Our only hope of finding peace and direction when we're out of our comfort zone is to cling to the Lord! He has much to teach us. He has much to say. Unfortunately, sometimes we can only hear Him when we are removed from our familiar surroundings. As we walk closely with Him, He speaks to us and lights our path.

Why is it so difficult to hear God in your everyday life? Busyness and distractions abound. The tyranny of the urgent keeps you running. Sensory overload is rampant. TV, Facebook, Twitter, the computer—so many voices drown out God's gentle whisper. The challenge is to desire to turn down the volume on worldly noises so that you can hear His voice speak to your heart. Begin your own journey today in learning how to listen to God. It's a choice you will never regret!

What noises drown out God's voice in your life? Are there any steps that you could take to begin a journey of listening to God more consistently? Ask the Lord to help you draw close to Him.

The Good Shepherd

*"My sheep hear my voice,
and I know them, and they follow me."*

JOHN 10:27

God audibly spoke to individuals and prophets in the Old Testament to fulfill His purposes. He instructed Noah to build an ark, Abraham to leave Ur, and Moses to lead the Israelites out of Egypt. Thousands of years later, Jesus was born and verbally communicated to those on earth. Before His death and resurrection, Jesus told His disciples that He must leave in order to have the Holy Spirit come. The Holy Spirit is Jesus' presence in every believer. He is our counselor and helper and teaches us all things (see John 14).

God may not speak audibly today, but He still speaks. As Christians, we are assured that Jesus is our Good Shepherd. He knows us and we can know Him. Ours is an intimate relationship where communication goes back and forth. As His sheep, we can learn to discern His voice so that we can follow Him. We have the indwelling Holy Spirit who guides us into all truth. The Holy Spirit gives us spiritual insight while we read the Bible and also speaks to our hearts in a still, quiet voice.

But you must be one of Jesus' sheep by faith in order to hear Him. The Good Shepherd laid down His life for you. He died so that you can be forgiven and have eternal life. When you receive Jesus by faith, you become one of His sheep. "For God so loved the world, that he gave his only Son, that whoever believes in him should not perish but have eternal life" (John 3:16). If you have not made that decision, why wait? Your Creator knows you inside and out. He desires that you know Him also! Become one of His sheep. Hear His voice so that you can follow. Start this incredible journey today!

Do you know the Good Shepherd personally because you've received Jesus as your Savior? Do you believe that He can speak to your heart? Have you ever discerned His voice and followed Him?

God Speaks

All Scripture is breathed out by God and profitable for teaching, for reproof, for correction, and for training in righteousness, that the man of God may be complete, equipped for every good work.

2 TIMOTHY 3:16–17

One day a Hindu teenager in Nepal picked up a Christian tract off the dirt road in his village. The booklet challenged him to choose between two roads—one narrow, the other wide. Curious about what that meant, he decided to attend church with a friend. Weeks later, he had a vivid dream of a man walking on water toward him saying, *"I am the way."* The next day he sought the counsel of the church pastor. When told the dream, the pastor immediately responded, "That was Jesus and He is coming for you!" Immediately the Nepali teenager received Jesus as his personal Lord and Savior!

Divinely inspired dreams may not be as common in the United States as in third-world countries, but God is always speaking. He communicates in many ways—through the Bible, the indwelling Holy Spirit, other people, creation, music, and circumstances. In fact, God Almighty can speak any way He chooses. He even spoke through Balaam's donkey! (See Numbers 22:21–39.)

God speaks through His Word, the Bible. If you need to hear God speak audibly, read the Bible aloud! The Holy Spirit, Jesus' presence, indwells every Christian. He communicates by giving you thoughts based on the truth of His Word. The Holy Spirit is your comforter and counselor, illuminating your spiritual eyes to truth. God speaks truth to you through other people in your life. Creation shouts His praises and points you to Creator God (see Psalm 19:2). Music can also usher you into His presence. Whatever means the Lord uses to communicate, His voice is *always* consistent with scripture. Many times He speaks the same message in different ways to get your attention. Be aware. Be attuned.

Has God ever spoken to you? How? If you have never experienced God communicating with you, begin reading and meditating on the Gospel of John or the Psalms.

Relationship

And without faith it is impossible to please him, for whoever would draw near to God must believe that he exists and that he rewards those who seek him.

HEBREWS 11:6

Imagine being blindfolded with your child or spouse standing behind you. If they spoke your name, you would recognize their voice because you know them personally. God desires that type of intimate, personal relationship with us. That's why He sent His Son, Jesus, into the world. Jesus was fully God. But Jesus was also fully man, so He can relate to us. Jesus makes a relationship with our heavenly Father possible. In John 14:6 Jesus says, "I am the way, and the truth, and the life. No one comes to the Father except through me."

Our relationship with God begins when we accept Jesus as our Lord and Savior by faith. But God doesn't want our relationship to end there. That's just the beginning! Because God created each one of us, He knows us through and through. He not only sees our actions but also knows our thoughts and emotions. God knows all about us. He wants us to know Him as well—His character, attributes, passion, and heart. Close relationships involve two-way communication. What type of relationship would there be if one person did all the talking? We talk to God through prayer and He listens. He wants to speak to us and have us listen as well.

Your relationship with God grows deeper as you draw near to Him. You begin to learn to discern His voice and respond by listening. The more He speaks, the more you will know Him. The more you know Him, the more intent you listen and the more He speaks. Like your loved one standing behind you while you're blindfolded, you will begin to recognize His voice when He calls your name. Spiritual rewards are yours when you draw near to God.

Have you ever desired to have a close, personal relationship with God? How might you begin or continue that journey? How could you nurture that relationship?

Follow Him

And when he had finished speaking, he said to Simon, "Put out into the deep and let down your nets for a catch." And Simon answered, "Master, we toiled all night and took nothing! But at your word I will let down the nets." And when they had done this, they enclosed a large number of fish, and their nets were breaking.

LUKE 5:4–6

Peter (Simon) had been fishing all night and had come up empty-handed. Yet when Jesus asked him to let down his nets, Peter obeyed. The result? The nets were bursting at the seams with so many fish! Peter listened to Jesus because they had a relationship. When Peter obeyed, he was able to witness Jesus' deity. He then fell at His feet in worship. Afterward Jesus said to Peter, "Do not be afraid; from now on you will be catching men" (Luke 5:10). Peter immediately left everything to follow Him.

Jesus desires a personal relationship with us. Like sheep following their shepherd, Jesus knows that we cannot follow Him unless we first know Him. Once our relationship is established, He speaks so that we can follow where He is leading. Obedience enables us to grow closer to Jesus as we experience His strength and power at work in our lives.

Peter obeyed Jesus' request to let down his net even though it seemed silly and preposterous. When you read something in scripture that God is asking of you—forgive your brother, do not be anxious, love your enemies—you need to follow in obedience. It may seem impossible to you, but with God's help, nothing is impossible! Obedience produces blessing. Jesus illustrated the spiritual blessings that Peter would later experience as he fished for men by allowing Peter to see the physical abundance of the fish he caught. You may not always see the spiritual blessings, but rest assured, they are always present when you obey!

Is following God easy or difficult for you? What areas are especially hard? Has the Lord ever asked you to do something that seemed preposterous or impossible? Trust Him.

Go Tell

Sue had trusted Jesus as her Savior at fifteen years old. In college she was involved with Cru and began consistently reading her Bible. As a young married woman, Sue was active in Bible studies and church. For twenty years God had been preparing her to step out of her comfort zone. So when she heard about the Nicaraguan mission trip at church, Sue sensed God calling her to go. She responded to His voice in obedience. Why?

God wants us to be His hands and feet to a lost world. People everywhere desperately need the Lord. We can share His love with others so that they can know Him too! We may be the only Bible someone reads. It has been said that Christianity is just one beggar telling another beggar where to get food—in this case, spiritual food. Jesus is the Bread of Life. Second Corinthians 5:17–20 encourages us as Christ's ambassadors: "Therefore, if anyone is in Christ, he is a new creation. The old has passed away; behold, the new has come. All this is from God, who through Christ reconciled us to himself and gave us the ministry of reconciliation; that is, in Christ God was reconciling the world to himself, not counting their trespasses against them, and entrusting to us the message of reconciliation. Therefore, we are ambassadors for Christ, God making his appeal through us."

You can't share Jesus effectively if you're not following Him wholeheartedly. However, as you obediently follow Him, the Holy Spirit begins transforming your heart. You will transition from dwelling on yourself to seeing others through God's eyes. You will begin to desire that others experience God's love, forgiveness, presence, and power in their lives as you have. Share what God shows you. Shout what He whispers in your ear! Tell the world of His love.

What do you think it means to be an ambassador for Christ? Have you had the opportunity to tell others about Jesus?

Deny Yourself

Then Jesus told his disciples, "If anyone would come after me, let him deny himself and take up his cross and follow me."

<small>MATTHEW 16:24</small>

Deny is a four-letter word in today's culture. Self-gratification permeates our society. We want something now and feel that we deserve it. So we obtain it. Whether it's buying the latest electronic gadget or climbing the corporate ladder, we will not be denied. To deny ourselves is countercultural. Yet that is exactly what Jesus is commanding us to do in order to follow Him.

Jesus warned His disciples that following Him would mean sacrifice and perseverance. Although this narrow road would lead to life, it would not be easy (see Matthew 7:13–14). They would suffer, yet by putting God's will above their own, they would become His disciples. Their lives would be radically changed and transformed. Others would be able to see Jesus living in and through them and come to believe in Him as well.

You too must deny yourself if you want to truly be a

disciple of Jesus. Defer to Him, and desire His will above your own. Denial is difficult but not impossible if you rely upon His strength. There might be things that you want, but God knows your true needs. He will provide and meet those needs. Trust Him. Pray about everything. Matthew 6:33 says, "But seek first the kingdom of God and his righteousness, and all these things will be added to you." Following Jesus is countercultural—radical even. Yet as you do, your heart is transformed from the inside out. As others observe this change, hopefully they will desire to know Jesus too.

Do you find it easy or difficult to deny yourself? What things do you struggle with? Do you sense that there is an area in your life where Jesus wants you to follow Him, yet you are clinging to your own will? Ask Him to help you let go and follow Him.

What are the advantages of being a disciple of Jesus? Have others noticed the change He has made?

Meddling with God

*And Sarai said to Abram, "Behold now, the L*ORD*
has prevented me from bearing children. Go in to my
servant; it may be that I shall obtain children by her."
And Abram listened to the voice of Sarai.*

GENESIS 16:2

God promised Abram that He would make him into a
great nation. There was only one problem: Abram was
childless. After waiting for more than ten years, Sarai,
Abram's wife, became impatient and came up with a plan.
Sarai decided that Abram could father a child through
her servant Hagar. Bad idea! Hagar became pregnant and
despised Sarai. Abram was caught in the middle of family
dysfunction. Although Sarai had meddled with God's plan,
it could not be thwarted. Fourteen years later, Isaac was
born to Abraham and Sarah just as God had promised.

Waiting on the Lord is extremely difficult! Like Sarah,
we are tempted to take circumstances into our own hands
by "helping" God. Our plan may seem well thought out,
but if it's not God's plan, adverse consequences will result.
Meddling with God does not thwart His plan. "I know

that you can do all things, and that no purpose of yours can be thwarted" (Job 42:2). But running ahead of God does have its consequences.

God's plans are always best, and His timing is always perfect. The more you believe that, the easier it becomes to wait on Him. While waiting, trust that God is still working. Sometimes God calls you to carry out His will by doing something, but wait for the Lord's nudge before springing into action. Learn to listen to God. Until you get confirmation through the Holy Spirit, scripture, or believers, be still. Have confidence that God will make it clear when you are to proceed. Trust Him. Do not meddle. Be still. Wait. He will be faithful!

Have you ever meddled with God's plans? Describe the situation and the results. Read Isaiah 40:30–31 and list the advantages of waiting on God. Are you in the waiting phase now? Continue to pray and trust in His perfect plan and timing.

Freedom Can Be a Mixed Bag

For you were called to freedom, brothers. Only do not use your freedom as an opportunity for the flesh, but through love serve one another.

GALATIANS 5:13

Charlotte didn't see it coming. Her friends were so much fun. But over time she started smoking, drinking, and engaging in sexual promiscuity. Before she knew it, at eighteen, she was addicted to heroin and selling her body to sustain her habit. Little choices made over time had led her down a destructive path. Fortunately, she cried out for help. Jesus restored her and gave her a future full of hope.

Jesus Christ came to set us free—free from the penalty of sin, which is death, and free from the power of sin in our daily lives. We should value, honor, and treasure that freedom because it was bought at a great price, His death. Our freedom was purchased, not so that we could do anything we want, but so that we could be free to follow Him. "Or do you not know that your body is a temple of the Holy Spirit within you, whom you have from God? You are not your own, for you were bought with a price.

So glorify God in your body" (1 Corinthians 6:19–20).

Christ bought your freedom, but He has also given you free will to make wise choices or foolish ones. Free will is a huge responsibility. Small choices can eventually lead to big consequences. Be wise as you exercise your freedom. What choices are you making today that you may regret tomorrow? Are your decisions in line with God's truth? God's road is always the right choice. You are not forced to do the right thing or obey God. But when you choose to walk in His ways, your life will be blessed. You will not live a life of regret, but a life that glorifies God. So choose wisely!

Looking back on your life, do you see little choices that eventually led to undesirable consequences? Are there good choices that led to blessings over time?

Light to My Path

*Your word is a lamp to my feet
and a light to my path.*

PSALM 119:105

At the end of their Nepal mission trip, Patty and Tom trekked to Pikey Peak base camp with experienced guides to catch a glimpse of Mt. Everest. After trekking four days, Patty became weary as they approached base camp at 15,000 feet. With the sun descending, temperatures began dropping and winds increased. Although the narrow path was pitch dark, their headlamps enabled them to stay on the right path and arrive safely at their destination.

Walking down an unknown path in the dark is frightening. Obstacles can obstruct the way. Even staying the course is difficult when many divergent paths cross one another. Imagine if there was no light to illuminate our path as we walk down the road of life. How would we know the way? How many times would we trip and stumble? How would we have strength to persevere?

The Lord has given you light—Jesus, the Light of the World! "Again Jesus spoke to them, saying, 'I am the light of the world. Whoever follows me will not walk in darkness, but will have the light of life'" (John 8:12). Jesus, the ultimate trekking guide, walks with you! The path is known to Him. He leads so that you can follow. God has given you the Bible to light the way, enabling you to stay on His path for your life. Even when you encounter hardships along the way, His Word encourages you and gives you hope to persevere. Your final destination is the ultimate peak—heaven! Jesus Himself will lead you home, and His Word will guide you along the journey. Why would you start off the day in the dark? Allow His Word to illuminate your path today!

Do you feel like your path is dark or illuminated? God wants His Word to light your path daily, not just occasionally. How are you doing with this? Ask God to help you to be more consistent so that His light can guide you each day.

One-Sided Love

He said to him the third time, "Simon, son of John,
do you love me?" Peter was grieved because he said to
him the third time, "Do you love me?" and he said to
him, "Lord, you know everything; you know that
I love you." Jesus said to him, "Feed my sheep."

JOHN 21:17

Margaret had fallen head over heels for Gary in college and enjoyed his company. But as the relationship deepened, Margaret realized that Gary usually called the shots. Their activities revolved around his interests and agenda. She was doing all the giving while Gary was doing all the taking. Thankfully Margaret came to her senses before they walked down the aisle. She recognized that an intimate, healthy love relationship requires give-and-take from both parties.

Although the disciple Peter truly loved Jesus, on the night of Jesus' arrest, Peter vehemently denied Him three times. As the rooster crowed, Peter's heart was pierced with grief for betraying his Lord. After His resurrection, Jesus appeared to Peter and questioned him three times

226

about his love. Each time Peter affirmed his love, Jesus asked him to feed and tend His sheep. Jesus had forgiven Peter, but if Peter truly loved Jesus, he would be willing to obey Him. Love is an action word.

There is no question about Jesus' love for you. He died on the cross to demonstrate His everlasting, steadfast love. But is your love relationship with the Lord one-sided? Is it all about what God can do for you? How does God feel if you just use Him for your purposes? In John 14:15 Jesus said, "If you love me, you will keep my commandments." Talk is cheap. Love must be demonstrated or it's not love at all. Jesus asks, "Do you love Me?" Are you reciprocating His love through obedience? These are some sobering reflections. God yearns for a two-sided love relationship with you.

Would you say that you are guilty of receiving God's love yet not reciprocating it? Are you willing to demonstrate your love through obedience? Ask for His help.

The Blame Game

But let each one test his own work, and then his reason to boast will be in himself alone and not in his neighbor. For each will have to bear his own load.

GALATIANS 6:4–5

The blame game is as old as the hills! When Adam ate the forbidden fruit, God confronted him. Adam responded, "The woman whom you gave to be with me, she gave me fruit of the tree, and I ate" (Genesis 3:12). Although Adam blamed Eve, he also indirectly blamed God. Eve immediately passed the buck by blaming the serpent. No one took personal responsibility for their actions. Everyone had an excuse.

Human nature has not changed. Blaming others seems easier than confronting our own sin. We deceive ourselves by believing that someone else has caused us to do the wrong thing. James 1:13–15 states: "Let no one say when he is tempted, 'I am being tempted by God,' for God cannot be tempted with evil, and he himself tempts no one. But each person is tempted when he is lured and enticed by his own desire. Then desire when it has conceived gives birth to sin, and sin when it is fully grown brings forth death." We alone are personally responsible for the choices we make. Our sin is not someone else's fault. Denial is a coping mechanism that blinds us. We must own our sin before we can confess it.

Give God permission to open your spiritual eyes to accurately assess your actions and attitude. Test your own work. Ask God to remove any blinders and expose the sin that you're unable to see. Your sin is not someone else's problem. Don't buy the lie that they caused it. Take personal responsibility by owning your sin instead of playing the blame game. Then God can forgive, heal, and restore.

How has the blame game played out in your own life or in the lives of others? Has it ever had a happy ending? Ask God to show you where you need to take personal responsibility for your attitudes and actions.

Denying God's Power

Now to him who is able to do far more abundantly than all that we ask or think, according to the power at work within us, to him be glory in the church and in Christ Jesus throughout all generations, forever and ever. Amen.

EPHESIANS 3:20–21

We limit God by thinking change is impossible. "For nothing will be impossible with God" (Luke 1:37). God can do anything! He radically transforms lives by His power. Consider Saul before he became the apostle Paul. Would anyone have imagined that Saul would change? Yet when Saul met Jesus on the road to Damascus, he made a complete turnaround. Instead of throwing Christians into prison, he was willing to suffer in prison for Christ's sake!

God can transform anyone into a new creation. "Therefore, if anyone is in Christ, he is a new creation. The old has passed away; behold, the new has come" (2 Corinthians 5:17). God's forgiveness and power are available to all by faith in Jesus Christ. No sin is greater than God's love. Although Saul was a murderer, God transformed his heart and used him greatly to spread the Gospel throughout the entire world!

Do not give up on anyone—especially yourself! No one is beyond the reach of God's transforming power. How much power would it take to raise someone from the dead? God's power that works in you is the same power that raised Jesus from the dead (see Ephesians 1:15–21). Wow! Never give up hope. Don't write anyone off. Continue to pray for God's divine intervention. Change can happen by God's power! His glory shines through the drug abuser's testimony, the alcoholic's redemptive story, or the criminal's rehabilitation. But don't forget that His glory is also displayed in ordinary lives that surrender to His transforming power. Never deny God's power!

Have you ever felt that someone was beyond God's reach? Pray for that person, believing that nothing is impossible with God. Can you think of an example of God's transforming power in someone's life? Ask for His power to change your own heart.

Anxiety vs. Peace

Do not be anxious about anything, but in everything by prayer and supplication with thanksgiving let your requests be made known to God. And the peace of God, which surpasses all understanding, will guard your hearts and your minds in Christ Jesus.

PHILIPPIANS 4:6–7

If given a choice, most of us would choose peace over anxiety. Yet as we obsess over situations that are out of our control, anxious thoughts flood our minds. Fear of the future ties us in knots. We wring our hands, sob in our beds, and vent to our friends. There is a better way. We do not have to be anxious. Peace is possible. How?

Examine your heart to see if you secretly enjoy hanging on to worry. Does "drama" give you a sense of importance and self-worth? When you refuse to obey this verse, you are choosing anxiety over peace. God does not want you to be anxious about *anything*! Pray instead of mulling over your thoughts and emotions. Jesus encourages, "Come to me, all who labor and are heavy laden, and I will give you rest. Take my yoke upon you, and learn from me, for

I am gentle and lowly in heart, and you will find rest for your souls. For my yoke is easy, and my burden is light" (Matthew 11:28–30).

Jesus wants to take your anxiety and stress and give you His peace in return. He alone can give you rest. The peace He imparts will guard your heart (emotions) and mind (thoughts). It is unexplainable. Thank God for listening, caring, and answering. The next time you feel anxious, you have a choice to make: hold on to anxiety or trade it for God's peace. Choose peace over anxiety today!

Would you say that anxiety or peace most characterizes your life? What things are you anxious or worried about? Have you ever obeyed this verse in Philippians? If so, what were the results? Was God faithful? Anxious thoughts have a way of creeping back over time. What should you do when that happens?

No Regrets

For godly grief produces a repentance that
leads to salvation without regret,
whereas worldly grief produces death.

2 CORINTHIANS 7:10

We all have regrets: a harsh word spoken, an unforgiving spirit, a rebellious heart. We can't go back and change the past, but we can learn from it. No one is perfect. Even the apostle Paul abhorred his behavior. "For I do not understand my own actions. For I do not do what I want, but I do the very thing I hate" (Romans 7:15). We can all relate!

Regrets and sin are bedfellows. Where you have one, you will have the other. Disobedience produces regret, whereas obedience produces blessing. But God knows that our deepest regrets can lead us to repentance, which in turn can lead us to Jesus. "If we confess our sins, he is faithful and just to forgive us our sins and to cleanse us from all unrighteousness" (1 John 1:9). Jesus forgives our sins and leads us to a future full of hope and promise.

If you want a life of no regrets, purpose to walk in

God's ways and follow Him in obedience. Forgive when it's difficult. Extend grace when it's undeserved. Love when it's hard. We will never regret doing those things. If you are a Christian, Jesus is with you forever in the presence of the Holy Spirit. As you walk in the Spirit and not in the flesh, regrets will characterize your life less and less. You will be transformed into the image of Christ more and more. Paul acknowledges that Christ is his only hope of living a life of no regrets (see Romans 7:24–25). The same is true for you. Walk in the power of the Holy Spirit each day.

What regrets do you have? Have you talked to the Lord about them? He wants to set you free from lamenting your past mistakes. Pray to receive His forgiveness and peace. What steps might you take to experience fewer regrets in life? Are there areas where Christ is calling you to obedience? Follow Him.

A Lighted Path

Your word is a lamp to my feet
and a light to my path.

PSALM 119:105

Paula met Mark through an online dating service. They seemed like the perfect match—both loved dogs, sports, and travel. Yet now, less than a year after their wedding, Mark had been unfaithful and shattered all of Paula's dreams. She felt hopeless and utterly alone as the darkness pressed in upon her.

Storms in life can rock or even capsize our boats in an instant. Our future looks bleak because our situation seems overwhelming and our emotions are reeling. Because of the pain that has overtaken us, we can't imagine ever experiencing joy again. All hope is gone. How do we take the next step into a future that looks so dark?

Cling to truth: God is with you. You are never alone. "It is the LORD who goes before you. He will be with you; he will not leave you or forsake you. Do not fear or be dismayed" (Deuteronomy 31:8). The future may look dark to you, but not to God. He has provided a lamp for your feet that will light your path—His Word. Cling to His promises, and believe that God has a plan for you and can bring beauty from ashes. Read the Bible daily, and allow His Word to illuminate your path. Psalms is a great place to find encouragement and peace. The Gospel of John leads us into the heart of Jesus, the Light of the World. Pray continually. God will show you the path forward one step at a time. He will be faithful to you. You *will* see a brighter day. When the sun shines again, you will know that God's Word and Jesus Himself were leading you in the darkness.

Has your world ever been shattered and left you feeling alone in the dark? Look up these verses and meditate on them: Romans 8:28–39; Jeremiah 29:11–14; Isaiah 43:1–3. Are you in the habit of reading the Bible daily? If not, ask God to help you.

Aging Gracefully

Gray hair is a crown of glory;
it is gained in a righteous life.

PROVERBS 16:31

Meg and Paige vowed to age gracefully and resist having face-lifts, Botox injections, and silicone implants. But over the years peer pressure intensified as their wrinkles stood in stark contrast to their friends' flawless complexions. At this rate, they would look like eighty-year-olds in no time! Was aging gracefully just an illusion? Believers are not exempt from societal pressure that values outward beauty and youth.

The Bible has much to say about what we should value. When Samuel came to anoint the next king of Israel, God reminded him, "For the LORD sees not as man sees: man looks on the outward appearance, but the LORD looks on the heart" (1 Samuel 16:7). First Peter 3:3–4 says, "Do not let your adorning be external—the braiding of hair and the putting on of gold jewelry, or the clothing you wear—but let your adorning be the hidden person of the heart with the imperishable beauty of a gentle and quiet spirit, which in God's sight is very precious."

God is more concerned with your heart than with your wrinkles. So focus more on your inner rather than your outward self. That doesn't mean that you let yourself go. You are to be a good steward of your body—eat healthy, exercise, and get adequate sleep. But embrace the wisdom that age has brought. Value what God values in you. Thank the Lord for the years that He has given you. Ask Him to help you navigate the road to aging gracefully with confidence as you concentrate more on your inner beauty. Dismiss worldly values by embracing what God values. See yourself as He sees you—beautiful on the inside and out!

Have you ever felt pressure to look younger or to be more attractive? How have you responded? How do you deal with peer pressure in this area, and where do you draw the line? Do you know an elderly person whose beauty radiates from within? What can you glean from them?

Temptation

No temptation has overtaken you that is not common to man. God is faithful, and he will not let you be tempted beyond your ability, but with the temptation he will also provide the way of escape, that you may be able to endure it.

1 CORINTHIANS 10:13

Melissa and Mike were exhausted physically, emotionally, and mentally. It was an opportune time for Satan's ambush. The father of lies launched his attack in Melissa's mind: *Mike doesn't really care about you. He doesn't protect you like a husband should.* Melissa began pondering those lies. She felt a sudden shift in her thinking as she began questioning her husband's love. An argument ensued as accusations were hurled. Melissa had taken Satan's bait.

Satan attacks when we are most vulnerable. "Be sober-minded; be watchful. Your adversary the devil prowls around like a roaring lion, seeking someone to devour" (1 Peter 5:8). Be aware when you feel most at risk. Satan tempted Jesus in the wilderness when He was hungry and alone. Be aware that we are in a spiritual battle (see

Ephesians 6:12). Because Satan is the father of lies, lying is his native tongue (see John 8:44). He uses lies to bait us. Sometimes his lies come disguised as half-truths, but they are still lies.

Although you have an enemy, God has given you victory in Jesus. You have been given spiritual armor (see Ephesians 6:13–18). The Holy Spirit resides within you to lead you into truth. Bank tellers handle real money constantly, so they are adept at immediately spotting counterfeits. In the same way, when you handle God's truth daily, you can best discern Satan's lies. Pray when you feel vulnerable. Look for your way of escape, and then take it! Do not give Satan a foothold. Resist him and he *will* flee from you. He knows that he has been defeated. Resisting him declares that truth!

When are you most vulnerable to Satan's attacks? Are there recurrent lies that Satan feeds you? Ask for discernment and for God's truth to speak louder.

It's Not a Contest

*Blessed be the God and Father of our Lord Jesus
Christ, the Father of mercies and God of all comfort,
who comforts us in all our affliction, so that we may
be able to comfort those who are in any affliction,
with the comfort with which we ourselves
are comforted by God.*

2 CORINTHIANS 1:3–4

Tony and Jackson had been close friends since college.
Now they both had entered a season of pain. After battling cancer for years, Tony's wife had recently passed
away. Jackson's son had checked into a drug rehab facility.
Jackson attempted to comfort Tony by saying, "What I'm
going through is nothing compared to losing your wife."
Tony responded, "Thanks, but both of us are hurting. It's
not a contest."

Pain is the same. Afflictions are part of life. It's easy
to become introspective, focusing on our overwhelming
circumstances and concluding that no one else is experiencing the same degree of difficulty. If we're not careful,
we can take on a martyr complex. Feelings of hopelessness

and despair can invade our emotions.

Don't try to weather the storm alone. God yearns to impart peace when your world seems to be falling apart. As you cry out to Him in your affliction, He will extend mercy and comfort you. God allows you to experience storms in life, but not for the purpose of bringing you down. Trials can strengthen and mature your faith as you steadfastly persevere. "Count it all joy, my brothers, when you meet trials of various kinds, for you know that the testing of your faith produces steadfastness. And let steadfastness have its full effect, that you may be perfect and complete, lacking in nothing" (James 1:2–4). Not only does God strengthen your faith through trials, but you can be used to bring comfort to others. Testify how God comforted you, and reassure others that God will surely meet their needs as well.

Has your faith ever matured through trials?
Has God's comfort sustained you? Have you been
able to share that hope with someone
else in their time of need?

Joy

Joy is rooted in spiritual reality. It is rock solid because it is based upon the finished work of Jesus Christ. Unlike happiness, joy is not determined by circumstances of life. In fact, true joy can be experienced in the darkest hours. The apostle Paul penned Philippians from jail. Joy filled his heart as he anticipated being ushered into heaven one day. Paul encouraged the Philippians, "Rejoice in the Lord always; again I will say, rejoice" (Philippians 4:4). How is that even possible?

Joy is a decision. Paul's joy was rooted in choosing to focus on his relationship with Jesus. Although Paul was in jail and had lost many things, he still had Jesus, the source of his joy. Paul demonstrated that joy can be experienced in the direst situations. If we know Jesus, nothing and no one can ever take Him away! Jesus promises in John 10:27–28: "My sheep hear my voice, and I know them, and they follow me. I give them eternal life, and they will never perish, and no one will snatch them out of my hand."

Circumstances are temporary. Your relationship with Jesus is permanent! Although it is hard, decide not to focus on your circumstances but on Him. Remember Peter walking on the water? He was fine until he took his eyes off Jesus and began looking at the wind and waves (see Matthew 14:22–33). In the storms of life, purpose to look at Jesus and not obsess about the difficult circumstances. Keep focused on Jesus by reading His Word daily and pouring out your heart to Him in prayer. When you do this, the joy of the Lord will indeed be your strength. May it be so, Lord Jesus!

What do you think is the difference between happiness and joy? Do you believe that it's possible to experience inner joy regardless of your circumstances? Has that ever happened to you? Please describe. Read and meditate on Romans 8:31–39. What could ever separate you from God's love?

Face the Giants

*"For the battle is the LORD's,
and he will give you into our hand."*

The battle lines were drawn between the Philistines and Israelites. Goliath, a Philistine, issued a challenge to any Israelite who would dare fight him to the death. If he won, the Israelites would become their slaves. But if an Israelite defeated Goliath, the Philistines would become slaves. Goliath stood nearly ten feet tall! Fear and trepidation filled the Israelites' hearts, with the exception of David, the shepherd boy. David was incensed that Goliath was defying the armies of the living God. He was confident that God's power would give him victory. David ran quickly toward Goliath, took a single stone from his pouch, slung it, and struck Goliath dead (see 1 Samuel 17).

David was confident that the Lord had prepared him for this battle. He had fought lions and bears while protecting his sheep. Yet he didn't trust in his own abilities but in the Lord Almighty's. David knew that this battle belonged to the Lord. Putting aside any fear, David boldly faced the giant. God defeated the enemy and gave the victory.

Instead of fleeing your giants, you must face them. Just as God equipped David with a small stone, He has equipped you with spiritual armor to defeat the giants in your life. You have the belt of truth and the breastplate of righteousness. Your shoes bring the gospel of peace. The shield of faith and helmet of salvation equip you to stand. Your offensive weapon is the sword of the Spirit, the Word of God (see Ephesians 6:10–17). God is in the business of fighting for you and giving you victory! Put on your armor and do not shrink back. "In all these things we are more than conquerors through him who loved us" (Romans 8:37).

Have you ever let fear cause you to run away from challenges in life? What if you decided to face those giants with God's strength? Ask Him to give you the boldness and confidence to do so. May His victory be yours today!

As You Will

"My Father, if it be possible, let this cup pass from me; nevertheless, not as I will, but as you will."

MATTHEW 26:39

A tragic car accident left one young man dead and another in a coma. Adam survived the accident and emerged from the coma, but trauma to his brain left him with severe disabilities. Four years later, although Adam is aware of his circumstance and fights to make progress, he remains dependent upon others for his daily care. Adam's parents have adapted their life to accommodate his need. They love and care for him every day.

Adam's parents have prayed for full restoration, asking God for a miraculous recovery. Yet progress has been limited. Has God failed to answer their prayers? On the contrary, Adam's parents have found peace and strength as they have discovered God's love in new circumstances, and they have felt God's presence ministering to them in ways they could not have imagined.

Can we change God's mind? How often, when we are hurting or discouraged, do we pray and ask God to remove our pain? It is only natural and He is certainly able. But changing God's mind may not be our best course. Instead, we may need to allow God to change *our* mind. In the Garden of Gethsemane, Jesus could see the pain He would soon face. He told His disciples, "My soul is very sorrowful, even to death" (Matthew 26:38). Then he submitted to His Father's will. Jesus serves as our example. In prayer, our ultimate goal is not to align God's will with ours, but to align our will with His. In the storms of life, submit to the heavenly Father's will and enter into the peace and strength found only in His presence.

When you pray, are you seeking a particular outcome? Or are you willing to trust God to answer your prayers according to His will for your life? Have you experienced, or witnessed in someone else, spiritual growth in the hard times when questioning God's presence or concern for your pain?

Dry Bones

*"Thus says the Lord GOD to these bones: Behold,
I will cause breath to enter you, and you shall
live. . . . And you shall know that I am the LORD."*

EZEKIEL 37:5–6

Ezekiel was among the Jews exiled to Babylon by Nebuchadnezzar in 597 BC. God called Ezekiel as a prophet to relay messages to His people regarding His divine judgments as well as their coming restoration and spiritual renewal. In Ezekiel 37:1–14, God brings Ezekiel to a valley of dry bones and instructs him to prophesy His Word to these bones. As Ezekiel obeyed, right before his very eyes, God Almighty raised these dry bones back to life! They stood strong and vibrant on their feet—a vast army!

Sometimes the Lord takes us to places of dry bones—a loss, a fractured relationship, or financial upheaval. He allows these dry, dead places in our lives for His purposes. Ezekiel saw *many* bones that were *very* dry. Our sorrows in life can seem this way too: numerous and hopeless.

When God asked Ezekiel if there was any hope that these bones could live, Ezekiel acknowledged that only

God could bring hope. The same is true for the dry bones in your life. There is hope that God can restore and bring life from death. Ezekiel obeyed and spoke God's Word. As you immerse yourself in God's Word, you'll be reminded of His power and promises. Peace and hope will be yours as you walk in God's truth. Just as God's words brought healing and life back into the dry bones, His Word will revive your life as well. When you are restored, you will know that God is the One who breathed His life into you! There is no hope or life apart from God Almighty.

Where does God need to revive the dry bones in you? Nothing is beyond God's power and ability to restore and bring back to life. Open His Word and receive hope for today.

Deep Calls to Deep

Deep calls to deep at the roar of your waterfalls;
all your breakers and your waves have gone over me.

PSALM 42:7

In 1869 Charles Spurgeon delivered a sermon titled "Deep Calls unto Deep." King David used this metaphor to describe his own sorrow when he penned this psalm. Spurgeon points out amazing harmonies in nature: storms stir up the oceans below and the heavens answer by sending rain. May the following excerpts from Spurgeon's sermon bring you hope.

> My brothers and sisters who have done business in the great waters, yours has been a stormy and tried life. . . . If in your experience there is a deep of extraordinary trial, there is most surely another deep answering to it. . . . In proportion to your tribulations shall be your consolations! If you have shallow sorrows, you shall receive but shallow graces, but if you have deep afflictions, you shall obtain the deeper proofs of the faithfulness of God! . . .

Great deeps of trial bring with them great deeps of promise! . . . Trials are mighty enlargers of the soul! . . . A great adversity will bring with it great grace to the believer. Whenever the Lord sets His servants to do extraordinary work, He always gives the extraordinary strength, or if He puts them to unusual suffering, he will give them unusual patience. . . . Don't forget that there is another deep, whose remembrance will remove from you the bitterness of your present sorrow—there is love in heaven towards you which will never grow cold—immortal and unchanging love! And besides, there is a royal oath which never can be broken, a covenant ratified with blood that never can be dishonored! You must be helped through—you cannot be left; God might sooner cease to be than cease to be faithful![1]

Have you ever cried out to God for comfort in times of deep suffering? Has God been faithful to you? If you are experiencing trials right now, be assured that He is able to meet your deepest needs.

1. C. H. Spurgeon, "Deep Calls unto Deep" (Sermon, Metropolitan Tabernacle, Newington, England, April 11, 1869).

After the Storm

And after you have suffered a little while, the God of all grace, who has called you to his eternal glory in Christ, will himself restore, confirm, strengthen, and establish you. To him be the dominion forever and ever. Amen.

1 PETER 5:10–11

Job was a righteous man who enjoyed prosperity and his family as he walked with God. And even after it was all taken away, he still worshipped God. "Then Job arose and tore his robe and shaved his head and fell on the ground and worshiped. And he said, 'Naked I came from my mother's womb, and naked shall I return. The LORD gave, and the LORD has taken away; blessed be the name of the LORD.' In all this Job did not sin or charge God with wrong" (Job 1:20–22). "The LORD blessed the latter days of Job more than his beginning" (Job 42:12).

In the midst of life's storms, our emotions make it difficult to imagine that we'll ever experience sunny days again. But the storm will eventually pass. Life is made of both storms and sunny days. What's the best way to handle both?

Jesus encourages you to abide in Him. Allow the indwelling Holy Spirit to guide you, teach you, and direct your steps. Glean truth from the Bible on a daily basis. Be still so that the Good Shepherd can speak to your heart. Before Jesus' death and resurrection, He comforted His disciples: "I have said these things to you, that in me you may have peace. In the world you will have tribulation. But take heart; I have overcome the world" (John 16:33). In Jesus we can have peace—regardless of our circumstances. Never give up hope. Jesus will restore you! The sun will shine again and God's rainbow will be seen in your life. Then God will use you to encourage someone else with His truth that sustained you!

Is it difficult for you to believe that the storm you are in will pass? Trust God to calm your emotions and give you hope. May His peace sustain you until the storm passes.

About the Author

Julie Rayburn is a Christian author and speaker. Her passion is to encourage and inspire the application of biblical truth. Her last book, *Be Still and Know: 365 Days of Hope and Encouragement for Women*, was inspired by a journal that her mother kept the last year of her life. *Peace in the Storms of Life* was birthed from Julie's own life experiences. Jesus was the calm in the center of her storms. As she called to Him from the depths of her soul, He answered. These devotionals are the spiritual insights she gleaned as she clung to biblical truth and listened to the Lord. She hopes that her readers will experience the peace that passes all understanding as they meditate on God's Word in the storms of life.

Julie has served as teaching director and area director for Community Bible Study (CBS). Currently, she and her husband, Scott, are serving as CBS ambassadors to Nepal. She is also on the CBS Board of Trustees.

Julie is a retired surgical orthopedic nurse. She enjoys tennis, golf, and gardening. Scott and Julie have two grown children and four grandchildren. They reside in the Atlanta area. Visit www.julierayburn.com.